Personality Plus

Personality Plus

Divya Chopra

4735/22, Prakash Deep Building,
Ansari Road, Daryaganj,
New Delhi - 110002

Lotus Press : Publishers & Distributors
Unit No. 220, 2nd Floor, 4735/22, Prakash Deep Building,
Ansari Road, Darya Ganj, New Delhi- 110002
Ph.: 23280047, 98118-38000
• E-mail : lotuspress1984@gmail.com
www.lotuspress.co.in

Personality Plus

ISBN: 978-81-8382-224-4

Printed & Published by : **Lotus Press Publishers & Distributors,** New Delhi-02

PREFACE

The development of a pleasing personality start with taking inventory of your habits with a view to change the bad ones and replace them with better habits and make improvements in your good habits. This should be a continuous process.

It is important to be considerate of others. Being genuinely interested in other people and respecting their dignity is one sure way to develop a pleasing personality, the personality that attracts.

Give others the chance to speak and listen to the other people's views. Do not bore others with tales of your problems and misfortunes. Do not minimise other people's achievements or try to press too much in making yourself look too important in their eyes. Do not gossip or collaborate with gossipers. Instead develop the habit of passing compliments.

Enthusiasm also aids in the cultivation of a pleasing personality. Above all, observe the golden rule; treat others as you would like to be treated. If you treat others the way you would like to be treated, you will not worry about whether people like you or not.

Author

CONTENTS

QUOTES ON THE PERSONALITY

All I need is my brains, my eyes and my personality, for better or for worse.

William Albert Allard

Personality is only ripe when a man has made the truth his own.

Soren Kierkegaard

If you have anything really valuable to contribute to the world it will come through the expression of your own personality, that single spark of divinity that sets you off and makes you different from every other living creature.

Bruce Barton

Personality has power to uplift, power to depress, power to curse, and power to bless.

Paul Harris

Man's main task in life is to give birth to himself, to become what he potentially is. The most important product of his effort is his own personality.

Erich Fromm

Don't try to take on a new personality; it doesn't work.

Richard M. Nixon

Personality is the glitter that sends your little gleam across the footlights and the orchestra pit into that big black space where the audience is.

Mae West

Show me an actress who isn't a personality and I'll show you a woman who isn't a star.

Katherine Hepburn

Personality is to a man what perfume is to a flower.

Charles Schwab

The most important function of education at any level is to develop the personality of the individual and the significance of his life to himself and to others.

Grayson Kirk

While one should always study the method of a great artist, one should never imitate his manner. The manner of an artist is essentially individual, the method of an artist is absolutely universal. The first personality, which no one should copy.

Oscar Wilde

The "self-image" is the key to human personality and human behaviour. Change the self-image and you change the personality and the behaviour.

Maxwell Maltz

The meeting of two personalities is like the contact of two chemical substances. If there is any reaction, both are transformed.

Carl Jung

CHAPTER 1

Personality: An Introduction

Many people mistake the physical appearance and various external characteristics of an individual and his or her personality. As they talk about a marvelous personality they may refer to the height, weight, stature and complexion. Well, if you think that it is just the appearance of the physique of a person that determines the personality, it is time to have a rethink. It is true that physical appearance does matter. However, since most of them are beyond our power and control, it is useless to waste our time and energy thinking on them. Though physical appearance can help, there are many other aspects that contribute greatly to one's personality.

Today, personality is considered the "Brand Image' of an individual. In simple terms, it is made-up of three aspects namely:

- Character
- Behaviour
- Attitude

Basically, personality development is the improvement of behaviour, communication skills, interpersonal relationships, attitude towards life and ethics. Character can be considered the basic factor in determining and individual's personality. There are several psychologists who say that improving character and behaviour alone will largely influence one's personality. It is a fact that all other factors behind a powerful personality will become useless if the person lacks a good character and behaviour.

Personality is like a building. Just as a building can exist only when it has a strong foundation, a personality can impress others only when it has a formidable basis. And the strong foundation is supplied by character and behaviour.

If personality is developed on the solid base of values and ethics, it will last forever. Fake smiles and mannerisms may attract others for a comparatively short period. However, they are shot-lived and do not help in improving one's personality.

Good behaviour and co-operation makes a man popular. As a result the possibilities of his progress and success are much more. Different people have different opinions about what makes a man's complete personality.

There are several scientists who have the view point that character does not form a part of personality, but Seven Covey, one of the all time great authors and motivators says the best personality should be based on the solid foundation of character.

The person who wants to improve his personality has to have a desire and determination; he has to identify the direction for his goals to achieve it. Once all the above three steps are taken he has to dedicate himself to the task of achieving his goal. Every human being is a unique creature. Therefore, in addition to the various common components, each one should develop his or her characteristics of personality. Always remember that blindly following someone else who is successful will never take you in the right direction.

There are immense possibilities within you to develop your personality with strong character you must recognise and understand them. The key to success is hidden with you. The wealth you have earned is not important but what is important, is the means you have adopted for acquiring that wealth. Your personality, your capabilities, your thoughts and your ideals are all very important in determining your character.

An individual's personality is an aggregate conglomeration of decisions we've made throughout our lives. There are inherent natural, genetic, and environmental factors that contribute to the development of our personality; however, in the pursuit of a more defined persona, many individuals enroll in courses offered in colleges to further or enhance the image they intend to project to others. These classes assist in identifying your conscious traits and contrasting them with what you intend to exhibit.

According to process of socialisation, "personality also colours our values, beliefs, and expectations...Hereditary factors that contribute to personality development do so as a result of interactions with the particular social environment in which people live." There are several personality types as Katharine Cook Briggs and Isabel Briggs Myers illustrated in several personalities typology tests.

These tests only provide enlightenment based on the preliminary insight scored according to the answers judged by the parameters of the test. Other theories on personality development are Jean Piaget stages of development, and personality development in Sigmund Freuid's theory being formed through the interaction of id, ego and superego.

Personality is defined as the enduring personal characteristics of individuals.

Although some psychologists frown on the premise, a commonly used explanation for personality development is the psychodynamic approach. The term psychodynamic describes any theory that emphasises the constant change and development of the individual. Perhaps the best known of the psychodynamic theories is Freudian psychoanalysis.

Freud's Psychoanalytic Theory

Drives

Freud believed that two basic drives – sex and aggression – motivate all our thoughts and behaviours. He referred to these as Eros (love) and Thanatos. Eros represents the life instinct, sex being the major driving force. Thanatos represents the death instinct (characterised by aggression), which, according to Freud, allowed the human race to both procreate and eliminate its enemies.

The Structure of Personality

Freud conceived the mind as only having a fixed amount of psychic energy. The outcome of the interaction between the id, ego and the superego (each contending for as much libidinal energy as possible) determines our adult personality.

The Tripartite Personality

Freud believed that personality had three parts– the id, ego, and superego– referring to this as the tripartite personality.

The id allows us to get our basic needs met. Freud believed that the id is based on the pleasure principle i.e. it wants immediate satisfaction, with no consideration for the reality of the situation.

As a child interacts more with the world, the ego begins to develop. The ego's job is to meet the needs of the id, whilst taking into account the constraints of reality. The ego acknowledges that being impulsive or selfish can sometimes hurt us, so the id must be constrained. The superego develops during the phallic stage as a result of the moral constraints placed on us by our parents.

It is generally believed that a strong superego serves to inhibits the biological instincts of the id (resulting in a high level of guilt), whereas a weak superego allows the id more expression (resulting in a low level of guilt).

Defence Mechanisms

The ego having a difficult time trying to satisfy both the needs of the id and the superego, employs defence mechanisms. Repression is perhaps the most powerful of these. Repression is the act by which unacceptable id impulses (most of which are sexually related) are "pushed" out of awareness and into the unconscious mind. Another example of a defence mechanism is projection.

This is the mechanism that Freud used to explain Little Hans' complex. Little Hans is said to have projected his fear for his father onto horses, which is why he was afraid of horses.

Psychosexual Stages

Freud believed that at particular points in the child's

development, a single part of the body is particularly sensitive to sexual stimulation. These eurogenous zones are the mouth, anus and the genital region. At any given time, the child's libido is focused on the primary eurogenous zone for that age. As a result, the child has certain needs and demands that are related to the eurogenous zones for that stage.

Frustration occurs if these needs are not met, but, a child may also become overindulged, and so may be reluctant to progress beyond the stage.

Both frustration and overindulgence may lead to fixations some of the child's libido remains locked into that stage. If a child is fixated at a particular stage, the method of obtaining satisfaction that characterised that stage will dominate their adult personality.

Stages

Oral Stage (0-18 months)

This stage begins at birth, when the mouth is the primary source of libidinal energy. A child who is frustrated at this stage may develop an adult personality that is characterised by pessimism, envy and suspicion. The overindulged child may develop to be optimistic, gullible, and full of admiration for others.

Anal Stage (18 months-3 yrs)

The child's focus on pleasure on this stage is on eliminating and retaining faeces. This represents the conflict between the id, which derives pleasure from the expulsion of bodily wastes, and the super-ego which represents external pressure to control bodily functions.

If the parents are too lenient in this conflict, it will result in the formation of an anal expulsive character who is disorganised, reckless and defiant.

Conversely, a child may opt to retain faeces, thereby spiting his parents, and may develop into an anal retentive character who is neat, stingy and obstinate.

Phallic Stage (3-6 yrs)

During this stage, boys develop unconscious desires for their mother and become rivals with their father for her affection. This is reminiscent with Little Hans' case study. So the boys develop a fear that their father will punish them for these feelings (castration anxiety) so decide to identify with him rather than fight him.

As a result, the boy develops masculine characteristics and represses his sexual feelings towards his mother. This is known as the Oedipus complex.

During recent years, it is now believed that girls go through a similar process. This is called the electra complex. Freud believed that the resolution of this female conflict comes much later and is never truly complete.

Latent (6 yrs-puberty)

The latency period is not a psychosexual development as such, but a stage when sexual drives lie dormant. Freud saw latency as a period of unparalleled repression of sexual desires and eurogenous impulses.

Genital Stage (puberty onwards)

This stage begins at puberty, when sexual urges are once again awakened. Interest now turns to heterosexual relationships. The less fixation the child has in earlier stages, the more chance they have of developing a "normal" personality, and thus develop healthy meaningful relationships with those of the opposite sex.

Although many people view Freud's descriptions of personality development as pure fantasy, his ideas have endured and have had far reaching influences both in and outside psychology.

Freud has changed the way we think about the importance of childhood, and also made us aware of the unconscious elements of our psyche that are essential for development.

How Personality Distinguishes You from Others?

Have you ever wondered why one person differs from another? Why do some people always seem to be happy and friendly, while others are often seen to be grouchy and not much fun to be with? How is one person different from the rest?

There are actually several factors that set a certain person to be different from others. The way a person acts, the way he thinks, he impresses others and most of all, it's his personality that sets him apart.

What is Personality?

Personality defined, according to William C. Menninger is someone "all that person has been, is, and hopes to be." Another notable psychologist Ernest R. Hilgard describes personality as "the sum total of individual characteristics and ways of behaving which, in their organisation or patterning, describe an individual's unique adjustments to his environment.

To sum up all these definitions, personality therefore, is made up of your physical attributes, your thoughts, feelings, memories, reactions, experiences, your dreams, ambitions for the future as well as your wishes.

Every individual is unique when all the factors mentioned are considered. That is why the sum total of all your different characteristics, which you may have inherited, or gotten, from the influence in your surroundings all makes up who you are– your personality.

The Need to Study Personality

In our day-to-day lives, we come across different types of people. Some people we like, and some we don't. And some, we have no particular feelings about.

Though we have different feelings about different people we meet, still, we have to deal and get along with them. It is unlikely that we will associate only to those we like and ignore those we don't really feel being around with.

That's just not how it works? So in order to get along with others, even to those we are not much fond of; we need to understand personality development and how it could affect our relationship with others? It is also a must for us to understand ourselves, who we are first?

Understanding behaviour differences, emotional and personality development will help us improve our relationship with other people and at the same time enhance our own.

How Personality is Developed?

Our personalities are the products of many factors and conditions which we have inherited or which exist in our environment. No two persons, except identical twins, have the same heredity. No two persons react in the same way to their environment. Every personality is unique and makes the individual different from others.

Though hereditary may be a strong factor on how a personality is developed, one's environment also exerts a strong influence on personality. Personality formation starts during childhood and one's unique characteristics can be learned from his environment.

Healthy Personality Development

One thing that both our parents believe very strongly in is the biblical phrase, "Train up a child in the way he should go and when he is old he will not depart from it." Today we interpret their thinking as the belief that our morals, learned behaviours, and sense of self are formed in our adolescent years therefore it's important for parents to establish a solid bases from which their children can continue healthy personality development.

This thinking is formally defined by Erikson's eight stages of development:

- Trust *versus* mistrust
- Autonomy *versus* shame and doubt
- Industry *versus* inferiority
- Identity *versus* role confusion
- Intimacy *versus* isolation
- Generativity *versus* stagnation
- Ego integrity *versus* despair
- Resolving the ego crises

The second stage of development — autonomy *versus* shame and doubt — occurs during the preschool years. During this stage of development, children are taught the value of self-control. It is important for parents to recognise that at this stage, the child's first attempts at developing self-control may be crucial. For example, they might fall, wet themselves, or encounter other accidents.

Therefore for healthy development to take place, it's critical that children receive support and encouragement from their parents.

Parents who criticise and condemn or who overly control or protect their children, work against the child's normal development and will actually instil feelings of doubt and confusion in the child as to his/her ability to achieve.

Upon successful completion of this stage children will know the difference between right and wrong and consciously make the right behavioural choice the majority of the time.

■■■

CHAPTER 2

Personality: Growth and Development

Many of us wonder if Personality Development is possible considering the fact that many personality theories suggest that we are born with our personalities.

Personality is our psychological behaviour that affects the way handle people around us and the situations we encounter in life. You hear the term; he has a cool personality or he has a high temper personality.

Both descriptions attempt to describe the person's interaction with people and situations.

Our Personality is decided by three main factors:

1. Heredity of our genes,
2. Our Environment, and
3. The Situation we handle.

Heredity of our genes refers to how we were born. The genes we inherit from our biological parents play a big role in our personality and our personality development. Our physical facial attraction, gender, muscle, reflexes, energy levels, hair are all decided in the chromosomes of our genes.

What support the above are many researches. There is a famous study which covered more than a 100 separated twins at birth. This study found these twins drove the same car type and model, names their dogs the same names, take their vacation two thousands miles away from home within couple of blocks from each others! Other research found that children inherit shyness, fear and distress.

It is not surprising that the cultures in which we grow, play a big role in our personality and personality development. Think of yourself as an example. If you grow in a religion related culture, your principles in life would be different to a person who grows up in an non-religious culture. Your principles, ideology and way of dealing with other might follow what your religion teaches you.

This is different if religion is not part of your culture where you tend to gauge right and wrong based on other factors that are taught in religions. An interesting theory of personality development shows that the first born child in a family is more concerned with social acceptance, more ambitious, more hardworking, more cooperative, more dependent, more prone to guilt feelings, prone to anxiety, and less aggressive than the second and third child of the same family. This is another evidence of the effect of our environment on our personality development.

The above factors of our personality equation might give "stereo typing" people a breathing space. However, it is not meant, should they consider the third factor in our personality development; the situation we handle. This is because no matter what is the culture you were raised within and the genes you have, you personality development can improve if you handle the situation in a well educated manner. By this, we mean that no matter who you are, you can be trained to handle the same situation in the same way that another person who has different genes and cultural background handles the same situation.

This is why customer service agents are trained to handle customers in the same way. Their personality development training as a customer agent focuses on certain ways to handle angry customers, answer them in a certain way, learn their name at the beginning of the phone call, learn when to call the supervisor, learn how to manage anger. The language skills of these customer agents might be different, but they sometimes sound the same personality to all of us.

This is because their personality training intended to focus them on the same customer handling no matter what their home born personality is.

Big Five Personality Traits

In psychology, the "Big Five" personality traits are five broad factors or dimensions of personality developed through lexical analysis. This is the rational and statistical analysis of words related to personality as found in natural-language dictionaries. The traits are also referred to as the "Five Factor Model" (FFM). The model is considered to be the most comprehensive empirical or data-driven enquiry into personality. The five factors are: Openness, Conscientiousness, Extraversion, Agreeableness, and Neuroticism. The Neuroticism factor is sometimes referred to as Emotional Stability. Some disagreement remains about how to interpret the Openness factor, which is sometimes called "Intellect".

Each factor consists of a cluster of more specific traits that correlate together. For example, extraversion includes such related qualities as sociability, excitement seeking, impulsiveness, and positive emotions.

The Five Factor Model is a purely descriptive model of personality, but psychologists have developed a number of theories to account for the Big Five.

The Big Five factors and their constituent traits can be summarised as follows:

- **Openness:** Appreciation for art, emotion, adventure, unusual ideas, curiosity, and variety of experience.
- **Conscientiousness:** A tendency to show self-discipline, act dutifully, and aim for achievement; planned rather than spontaneous behaviour.
- **Extraversion:** Energy, positive emotions, and the tendency to seek stimulation and the company of others.
- **Agreeableness:** A tendency to be compassionate and cooperative rather than suspicious and antagonistic towards others.
- **Neuroticism:** A tendency to experience unpleasant emotions easily, such as anger, anxiety, depression, or vulnerability; sometimes called emotional instability.

When scored for individual feedback, these traits are frequently presented as percentile scores. For example, a Conscientiousness rating in the 80th percentile indicates a relatively strong sense of responsibility and orderliness, whereas an Extraversion rating in the 5th percentile indicates an exceptional need for solitude and quiet.

Although these trait clusters are statistical aggregates,

exceptions may exist on individual personality profiles. On average, people who register high in Openness are intellectually curious, open to emotion, interested in art, and willing to try new things.

A particular individual, however, may have a high overall Openness score and be interested in learning and exploring new cultures. Yet, he or she might have no great interest in art or poetry. Situational influences also exist, as even extraverts may occasionally need time away from people.

The most frequently used measures of the Big Five comprise either items that are self-descriptive sentences or, in the case of lexical measures, items that are single adjectives. Due to the length of sentence-based and some lexical measures, short forms have been developed and validated for use in applied research settings where questionnaire space and respondent time are limited.

Openness to Experience

Openness to experience is one of five major domains of personality discovered by psychologists. Openness involves active imagination, aesthetic sensitivity, attentiveness to inner feelings, preference for variety, and intellectual curiosity. A great deal of psychometric research has demonstrated that these qualities are statistically correlated. Thus, openness can be viewed as a global personality trait consisting of a set of specific traits, habits, and tendencies that cluster together.

Openness tends to be normally distributed with a small number of individuals scoring extremely high or low on the trait, and most people scoring near the average. People who score low on openness are considered to be closed to experience. They tend to be conventional and traditional in their outlook and behaviour.

They prefer familiar routines to new experiences, and generally have a narrower range of interests. They could be considered practical and down to earth.

People who are open to experience are no different in mental health from people who are closed to experience. There is no relationship between openness and neuroticism, or any other measure of psychological wellbeing. Being open and closed to experience are simply two different ways of relating to the world.

Sample Openness items:

- I am full of ideas.
- I am quick to understand things.
- I have a rich vocabulary.
- I have a vivid imagination.
- I have excellent ideas.
- I spend time reflecting on things.
- I use difficult words.
- I am not interested in abstract. (*reversed*)
- I do not have a good imagination. (*reversed*)
- I have difficulty understanding abstract ideas. (*reversed*)

Conscientiousness

Conscientiousness is the trait of being painstaking and careful, or the quality of acting according to the dictates of one's conscience. It includes such elements as self-discipline, carefulness, thoroughness, organisation, deliberation (the tendency to think carefully before acting), and need for achievement. It is an aspect of what was traditionally called character.

Conscientious individuals are generally hard working and reliable. When taken to an extreme, they may also be workaholics, perfectionists, and compulsive in their behaviour.

People who are low on conscientiousness are not necessarily lazy or immoral, but they tend to be more laid back, less goal oriented, and less driven by success.

Sample Conscientiousness items:

- I am always prepared.
- I am exacting in my work.
- I follow a schedule.
- I get chores done right away.
- I like order.
- I pay attention to details.
- I leave my belongings around. (*reversed*)
- I make a mess of things. (*reversed*)
- I often forget to put things back in their proper place. (*reversed*)
- I shirk my duties. (*reversed*)

Extraversion and Intervention

The trait of extraversion-introversion is a central dimension of human personality. Extraverts (also spelled *extroverts*) tend to be gregarious, assertive, and interested in seeking out excitement. Introverts, in contrast, tend to be more reserved, less outgoing, and less sociable.

They are not necessarily loners but they tend to have smaller circles of friends and are less likely to thrive on making new social contacts. Introverts are less likely to seek stimulation from others because their own thoughts and imagination are stimulating enough.

Extraversion and introversion are generally understood as a single continuum. Thus, to be high on one is necessarily to be low on the other. That said, people fluctuate in their behaviour all the time, and even extreme introverts and extraverts do not always act consistently.

Sample Extraversion items:

- I am the life of the party.
- I don't mind being the centre of attention.
- I feel comfortable around people.
- I start conversations.
- I talk to a lot of different people at parties.
- I am quiet around strangers. (*reversed*)
- I don't like to draw attention to myself. (*reversed*)
- I don't talk a lot. (*reversed*)
- I have little to say. (*reversed*)

Agreeableness

Agreeableness is a tendency to be pleasant and accommodating in social situations. In contemporary personality psychology, agreeableness is one of the five major dimensions of personality structure, reflecting individual differences in concern for cooperation and social harmony. People who score high on this dimension are on average more empathetic, considerate, friendly, generous, and helpful.

People scoring low on agreeableness place self-interest

above getting along with others. They are generally less concerned with others' well-being, report less empathy, and are therefore less likely to go out of their way to help others. Their skepticism about other people's motives may cause them to be suspicious and unfriendly. People very low on agreeableness have a tendency to be manipulative in their social relationships. They are more likely to compete than to cooperate.

Agreeableness is considered to be a superordinate trait, meaning that it is a grouping of more specific personality traits that cluster together statistically. There are exceptions, but in general, people who are concerned about others also tend to cooperate with them, help them out, and trust them. This dimension of personality was initially discovered in research using the method of factor analysis.

Agreeableness can be viewed as the opposite of machiavellianism. It is also similar conceptually to Alfred Adler's idea of social interest.

Sample Agreeableness items:

- I am interested in people.
- I feel others' emotions.
- I have a soft heart.
- I make people feel at ease.
- I sympathise with others' feelings.
- I take time out for others.
- I am not interested in other people's problems. (*reversed*)
- I am not really interested in others. (*reversed*)
- I feel little concern for others. (*reversed*)
- I insult people. (*reversed*)

Neuroticism

Neuroticism is a fundamental personality trait in the study of psychology. It can be defined as an enduring tendency to experience negative emotional states. Individuals who score high on neuroticism are more likely than the average to experience such feelings as anxiety, anger, guilt, and clinical depression.

They respond more poorly to environmental stress, and are more likely to interpret ordinary situations as threatening, and minor frustrations as hopelessly difficult. They are often self-conscious and shy, and they may have trouble controlling urges and delaying gratification.

Neuroticism is related to emotional intelligence, which involves emotional regulation, motivation, and interpersonal skills. It is also considered to be a predisposition for traditional *neuroses*, such as phobias and other anxiety disorders.

Sample Neuroticism items:

- I am easily disturbed.
- I change my mood a lot.
- I get irritated easily.
- I get stressed out easily.
- I get upset easily.
- I have frequent mood swings.
- I often feel blue.
- I worry about things.
- I am relaxed most of the time. (*reversed*)
- I seldom feel blue.(*reversed*)

Personality Development

Five Ways to Stay Focused on Your Goals

No matter how excited you are about your business, with so many distractions and things that may be going on in your life, you can easily find yourself losing focus on your goals and what you want to accomplish. Below you will find five things that will help you stay focused on your goals.

Finish What You Started

You probably have heard the saying, "So many things to do and not enough time to do them." Even though that may be true, you still have to complete them all, especially if these things help you to reach your goals. To make it easier for you, just take 1 thing you have to do and complete that task until it is done. When it is done, you will feel a sense of accomplishment and it will motivate you to move on to your next task.

Organise to make things Easy and Simple

Take a moment to put things in order. If people write to you or send you orders in the mail, make three piles. Put the letters that need to be answered right away in the 1st pile. Letters that can be answered at a later date you can put in the 2nd pile and letters that have orders in them, you can put in the 3rd pile. Doing things like this in other areas of your life will help you keep things in priority and keep you focused on your goals.

Change the Way You Look at Things

If you find yourself at times having a negative attitude, you must realize that the way you look at things can make all the difference when it comes to reaching your goals. Even when obstacles stand in your way, maintaining a positive attitude, not a negative one and knowing that things can and will get better, will help you stay on track in reaching your goals.

Understand Goals will take Time to Reach

Everything in life, if it is worth it, will take time. This goes for the goals you set for yourself. When you set goals, you should set two types of goals. A short-term goal such as six months and also a long range goal, such as three years. You must realize that you are not going to reach your long-term goals in two weeks. Whatever your goals may be, only through hard work, determination and keeping yourself focused, this is the way you will eventually reach your goals.

Stusy and Read Articles on Motivation

Reading articles, books or even listening to cassette tapes on motivation is a must if you want to keep yourself focused on your goals. Many successful people will tell you that even when they wanted to give up and throw in the towel, a paragraph in a book or something a motivational speaker said put them back on the right track and helped them reach their goals. So, if you want to stay focused on your goals, take these five points and put them into action today.

Can You Hear Yourself Lead?

Do you find days turning into weeks, which turn into years and suddenly you're not sure where it's all gone? Does it seem like your no longer navigating your own life but your life and your schedule are navigating you instead? Can you hear yourself lead? If this describes you, stop. Just stop. Stand still, be still, and let yourself remember what the silence feels like.

So often in the world we call business, we go so fast we

lose our ability to keep up when, in fact, keeping up is impossible. Simply put, if you're caught up, you're out of business. Business is the competitive pull and push that can kick our navigational system clean out of whack. To get back in control, you have to stop and listen.

We are taught to listen to everyone else. That listening is the greater asset. However, we are never taught to listen to ourselves. Creativity dies in the face of too much noise. Without creativity everything in your life suffers, including your business. Sometimes the most important person to listen to is you. Yes, you have something to say but if you never stop to listen you won't ever get back to navigating again.

So here's what you can do to put yourself back in the driver's seat :

1. Start the day by emptying your emotions into a journal. Let all the emotional garbage out on paper. Now, don't read it. Too hard to do? Rip it up and throw it away. This is just a tool to get the frustrations processed and out of your life so you can move on. So you can hear yourself think again. Sometimes our lives get filled up with everyone else's chatter. This helps us empty that out.
2. Take 15 minutes out of the middle of your day and rest. Just stop everything. Go to a room; take off the phone, the fax, the instant messenger and the ringer on your email. Find a place where you won't be bothered and stop. Take ten deep breaths. Let your mind empty. Try to spend at least five minutes of the fifteen thinking of nothing. Don't laugh, it's really hard to do. Think of nothing. Empty your brain and give your soul a rest.
3. Walk. Walking doesn't just exercise your body, it relaxes your soul. Walk with a friend, or walk alone, but walk. This

isn't about exercise, it's about letting your mind breath, outside, in the rain, in the sun, in the snow..in the fresh air. It works!

4. Okay, this is the most important. At the end of the day, spend another 15 minutes writing down all the advice that was given to you today. All those noteworthy, seemingly wise bits of advice that get hurled at us everyday. It doesn't matter where they came from, a book, a phone call, a radio station.. doesn't matter. If you can remember it write it down. Now read them all. Do any of them feel adverse to your own feelings and thoughts? Great, cross them out and forget them. Learn to trust that some things will work for you and some things won't. Once you have learned this principle you will find yourself getting back into the drivers seat of your own life again.

Remember you're important too and you are the only one that lives the results and consequences of your own life. Be gentle with yourself and take the time to take the time. Suddenly hours will screech back to normal speed, life will feel worth the effort, and your goals will be realized again.

Confidence

Every day is a new day in our life. There is much to do today. The early morning sun inspires us to start things freshly and put back our past. Only a handful of us make use of this fresh bunch of energy. In various walks of life this affects the way we behave and our confidence level. Confidence is a key to survive in this world. It is the only key tool to win the rat race in every walk of life. Confidence in ones own capabilities combined with sincere efforts helps one to achieve unthinkable heights. But many times we see that this basic element of confidence is missing in us. As a result of lack of confidence we perform well below our caliber. Be it in a public speech, proposing your beloved, vivas in your college or in an interview or say even on the eve before your exams. This can be due to fear of being rejected or any other reason.

If we look into our hearts and think, we will come to know that fear inside us is going to get us nowhere. The confidence inside us is going to take us places. This is because with confidence we can put our thoughts into words in a better and pleasing way. So we have to get out of that shell where we think whether people will accept us as we are? Instead of living in these unending moments of fear and thoughtless analysis it is better if we project ourselves with the skills we have with the gloss of confidence. With confidence we can portray the finer points of our personality in such a way that the places where we do lack are never highlighted.

Confidence should glow in us only till the point where our personality is boosted. Above this it leads to over-confidence that is harmful.

Over confidence results in unsatisfied performance levels as the seed of ego grows into a plant into our mind. We then imagine and make big talks just to maintain our ego. So guys don't let the seed of ego to germinate in your mind, as this seed should be used only for you to live up to your expectations.

Different Strokes of our Duties

Life teaches us to live. To live, you have to exist. To exist, you should have a passport to this living world. Thanks your parents, who brought you into this world.

Parents have taken care of us and satisfied all our needs.

They helped whenever we were hungry, afraid or ill. They were always there by you, whenever you needed them. You almost assumed that they will always be there for you and never thought of how your life would be without them. But as you grow up, age also catches up with your parents and they need your help and support.

Man is a child first, after which he attains his youth. After youth he again goes through the second phase of childhood, also called as old age. This is the phase where everyone needs a comfort of a sense of belonging and being taken care of. Wouldn't we all expect the same sense of security when we grow old?

Even our parents are expecting us to be their caretaker, as they grow old. But they never make that obvious to us. They do their further duty by taking care of their grandchildren, paying e-bills, giving the clothes for laundry etc.

Isn't it unfair on our part that we aren't giving them what they need the most? It is our prime duty to take the very best care of them. It's our pay back time. Lets give the same sense of emotional security, care and love to our parents in their old age.

Some of us mistreat our parents and consider them more of a liability than an asset. Some of us move away from them, though our conscience pricks us. We err in our duties for not being dutiful. This guilty feeling is further wrapped into a sense of regret, when we will be treated in the same way by our future generation. After all you only get what you deserve. Don't you?

Let's keep in mind that to be a manager, husband or father, we first have to be a son.

Motivate Yourself

One of the greatest virtues of human beings is their ability to think and act accordingly. The emergence of the techno savvy man from the tree swinging ape has really been a long journey. This transition has taken a span of countless centuries and lots of thinking caps have been involved. Inquisitiveness and aspiration to come out with the best have been the pillars for man's quest for development. Self-motivation is the sheer force, which pulled him apart and distinguished him from his primitive ancestors.

Many times, in our life, when we are reviving old memories we get into a phase of nostalgia. We feel that we could have done better than what we had achieved. Be it thinking about that nerve shattering school result, because of which you couldn't get into your favorite stream or that single mark, which could have secured you a merit seat in your engineering college. But thinking back wont rewind the tireless worker called time. All we can do is promise ourselves that we will give our very best in the future. But do we really keep up to our mental commitments? I can guess that 90% answers are in the negative. This is because of that creepy careless attitude which is slowly, but surely entering into the mind of teenagers like us. We easily forget the pains of yesterday to relish the joys of today. This is the only time in our life, when we can control our fate, by controlling our mind. So it is time to pull up our socks and really motivate ourselves so that we can give our best shot in the future. Self-motivation is the need of the hour. Only we can control and restrict ourselves. Its upto us, how we use our mental capabilities to the best of our abilities.

Here are some Funda's for self-motivation. Don't just read

them digest each one of them and apply them and I bet it will make a better you.

The ultimate motivator is defeat. Once you are defeated, you have nowhere to go except the top.

Then only thing stopping you is yourself.

There is no guarantee that tomorrow will come. So do it today.

Intentions don't count, but action's do.

Don't let who you are, stunt what you want to be.

Success is the greatest motivator.

Your goals must be clear, but the guidelines must be flexible.

Try to include these one liners in your scrapbook or on your favourite poster. You will be sub-consciously tuned to achieve what you want. Also do keep in mind that nothing can control your destiny but you!

The Power of Expressions

Expressions are a way of giving some life to the thoughts and feelings inside us. When you cry, u express sadness and disappointment. When you catch a good joke, you laugh a lot and express the pleasure.

Expressions are a part and parcel of every human being on this earth. Every person has the right to express himself. It is only through expressions that one can achieve a harmony between the physical exterior and the mental core. It is a way of giving life to your thoughts and feelings. But not everyone expresses freely. The main reasons are the barriers we have created within ourselves. We always think of what the world would think of us. Because of this we restrain ourselves from laughingly completely, tilting our head, or even scratching our ears! We try to be not what we are, but what we think will appeal to the world. Hardly do we realize that the world is just like us. It will be busy thinking of what we will think of it, rather than analyzing our actions.

When one expresses one self freely, it's the ultimate satisfaction for the mind. This is because the physical hardware of the human body is faithfully supporting its mental software. The person then is always comfortable anywhere with anyone and at anytime! If one doesn't express properly, it wont make the sun rise in the west, but it will only lead to increased frustrations. When frustrations increase, efficiency decreases and a person starts blaming the world, god or anyone in general.

Well to practically speak of expressions, once you start using them in your normal day to day life, u will get used to them. Also people around you will get used to your expressions. When the doyen of Indian film industry Mr. Amitabh Bachchan came into the movies, he had one eye smaller than the other. He however carried on without being self-conscious about it and captured the heart of countless Indians dead and alive. Also Sylvester Stallone, who is the famous Mr. Big Muscles from Hollywood was actually having some mental problems in his childhood. Even now look at his eyes and you will get a rare glimpse. But then he came above all that and now you can all see how big he has become.

If you are angry at some one, let him know. If you admire someone, let that person know. If you love someone, let her know, because life is too short to keep these things as secret. Express yourself and spice up your life.

Watch Out Before You Speak

Communication in any form is used for exchange of information. The links called words make communication work. Without words its difficult to imagine how we could have come so long in the history of human evolution. Word is not only a 4-letter thing, but it is something deeper than that.

Whenever a word is uttered it is due to synchronization of lip movement and tongue movement. To get out that word from our mouth, a lot of thinking and analysis has been happening in our sub conscious mind. We don't realize it because all this happens in less than one millionth of a second. Most of the times we don't think over what we have uttered. Word is not only a link, but it initiates response from the listener.

The word, which we have uttered, acts on every part of the listener's body. Like if u share a joke using a group of words, u make the listener to laugh. He may pound his hands and fist and then calm down. The very word which u have uttered has allowed him to flush his emotions out in the form of laughter or smile. If you talk about a tragic incident, the listener may close his eyes for a second and offer his condolences. Words uttered vibrate on the mind of the listener. It acts on his mind. Selection and thought prior to communication is very important.

Sometimes we say things which we shouldn't have or we carelessly utter unwanted words (mind you I am not talking of abuses). These things may affect the other person emotionally and mentally. For us it would have been just a matter of second to wag our tongue, but for the listener it is going to be the only thing at the back of his mind. By using unwanted words or speaking more than necessary, we not only hurt someone, but we also add a spot of dust to our social image. Your future interaction with the person may be based on that single word. Using proper words while talking is just like selecting the items listed out by your mom from the supermarket. You select the best brand from the specific domain, where your item is found.

So guys watch before you speak because the actions of the listener may be louder than your words!

Some Useful Steps in Personality Development

How to Win Friends and Influence People?

Fundamental Techniques in Handling People:

1. Don't criticise, condemn or complain.
2. Give honest and sincere appreciation.
3. Arouse in the other person an eager want.

Six ways to make people like you:

1. Become genuinely interested in other people.
2. Smile.
3. Remember that a person's name is to that person the sweetest and most important sound in any language.
4. Be a good listener. Encourage others to talk about themselves.
5. Talk in terms of the other person's interests.
6. Make the other person feel important - and do it sincerely.

Win people to your way of thinking:

1. The only way to get the best of an argument is to avoid it.
2. Show respect for the other person's opinions. Never say, "You're wrong."
3. If you are wrong, admit it quickly and emphatically.

4. Begin in a friendly way.
5. Get the other person saying "yes, yes" immediately.
6. Let the other person do a great deal of the talking.
7. Let the other person feel that the idea is his or hers.
8. Try honestly to see things from the other person's point of view.
9. Be sympathetic with the other person's ideas and desires.
10. Appeal to the nobler motives.
11. Dramatise your ideas.
12. Throw down a challenge.

Be a Leader: How to Change People without Giving Offence or Arousing Resentment.

A leader's job often includes changing your people's attitudes and behaviour. There are some suggestions to accomplish this:

1. Begin with praise and honest appreciation.
2. Call attention to people's mistakes indirectly.
3. Talk about your own mistakes before criticising the other person.
4. Ask questions instead of giving direct orders.
5. Let the other person save face.
6. Praise the slightest improvement and praise every improvement. Be "hearty in your approbation and lavish in your praise."
7. Give the other person a fine reputation to live up to.
8. Use encouragement. Make the fault seem easy to correct.
9. Make the other person happy about doing the thing you suggest.

How to Stop Worrying and Start Living?

Fundamental facts you should know about worry are:

1. If you want to avoid worry, do what Sir William Osler did: Live in "day-tight compartments." Don't stew about the futures. Just live each day until bedtime.
2. The next time Trouble—with a Capital T—backs you up in a corner, try the magic formula of Willis H. Carrier:

a) Ask yourself, "What is the worst that can possibly happen if I can't solve my problem?

b) Prepare yourself mentally to accept the worst—if necessary.

c) Then calmly try to improve upon the worst—which you have already mentally agreed to accept.

3. Remind yourself of the exorbitant price you can pay for worry in terms of your health. "Those who do not know how to fight worry die young."

Basic techniques in analysing worry:

1. Get the facts. Remember that Dean Hawkes of Columbia University said that "half the worry in the world is caused by people trying to make decisions before they have sufficient knowledge on which to base a decision."
2. After carefully weighing all the facts, come to a decision.
3. Once a decision is carefully reached, act! Get busy carrying out your decision—and dismiss all anxiety about the outcome.
4. When you, or any of your associates, are tempted to worry about a problem, write out and answer the following questions:

a) What is the problem?

b) What is the cause of the problem?

c) What are all possible solutions?

d) What is the best solution?

How to break the worry habit before it breaks you?

1. Crowd worry out of your mind by keeping busy. Plenty of action is one of the best therapies ever devised for curing "wibber gibbers."
2. Don't fuss about trifles. Don't permit little things—the mere termites of life—to ruin your happiness.
3. Use the law of averages to outlaw your worries. Ask yourself: "What are the odds against this thing's happening at all?"
4. Co-operate with the inevitable. If you know a circumstance is beyond your power to change or revise, say to yourself: "It is so; it cannot be otherwise."
5. Put a "stop-less" order on your worries. Decide just how much anxiety a thing may be worth—and refuse to give it anymore.
6. Let the past bury its dead. Don't saw sawdust.

Six ways to cultivate a mental attitude that will bring you peace and happiness:

1. Let's fill our minds with thoughts of peace, courage, health, and hope, for "our life is what our thoughts make it."
2. Let's never try to get even with our enemies, because if we do we will hurt ourselves far more than we hurt them. Let's do as General Eisenhower does: let's never waste a minute thinking about people we don't like.

a) Instead of worrying about ingratitude, let's expect it. Let's remember that Jesus healed ten lepers in one day—and only one thanked Him. Why should we expect more gratitude than Jesus got?

b) Let's remember that the only way to find happiness is not to expect gratitude—but to give for the joy of giving.

c) Let's remember that gratitude is a "cultivated" trait; so if we want our children to be grateful, we must train them to be grateful.

3. Count your blessings—not your troubles!
4. Let's not imitate others. Let's find ourselves and be ourselves, for "envy is ignorance" and "imitation is suicide."
5. When fate hands us a lemon, let's try to make a lemonade.
6. Let's forget our own unhappiness—by trying to create a little happiness for others. "When you are good to others, you are best to yourself."

The perfect way to conquer worry:

1. Prayer

How to keep from worrying about criticism:

1. Unjust criticism is often a disguised compliment. It often means that you have aroused jealousy and envy. Remember that no one ever kicks a dead dog.
2. Do the very best you can; and then put up your old umbrella and keep the rain of criticism from running down the back of your neck.
3. Let's keep a record of the fool things we have done and criticise ourselves. Since we can't hope to be perfect, let's do what E.H. Little did: let's ask for unbiased, helpful, constructive criticism.

Six ways to prevent fatigue and worry and keep your energy and spirits high:

1. Rest before you get tired.

2. Learn to relax at your work.
3. Learn to relax at home.
4. Apply these four good workings habits:
   a) Clear your desk of all papers except those relating to the immediate problem at hand.
   b) Do things in the order of their importance.
   c) When you face a problem, solve it then and there if you have the facts to make a decision.
   d) Learn to organise, deputise, and supervise.
5. To prevent worry and fatigue, put enthusiasm into your work.
6. Remember, no one was ever killed by lack of sleep. It is worrying about insomnia that does the damage—not the insomnia.

The Quick and Easy Way to Effective Speaking

Fundamentals of Effective Speaking are:

1. Acquiring the Basic Skills
   - Take heart from the experience of others
   - Keep your goal before you
   - Predetermine your mind to success
   - Seize every opportunity to practice
2. Developing Confidence
   - Get the facts about fear of speaking in public
   - Prepare in the proper way
   - Predetermine your mind to success
   - Act confident

3. Speaking Effectively the Quick and Easy Way
   - Speaking about something you have earned the right to talk about through experience or study
   - Be sure you are excited about your subject
   - Be eager to share your talk with your listeners

Speech, Speaker, and Audience

4. Earning the Right to Talk
   - Limit your subject
   - Develop reserve power
   - Fill your talk with illustrations and examples
   - Use concrete, familiar words that create pictures
5. Vitalising the Talk
   - Choose subjects you are earnest about
   - Relive the Feelings you have about your topic
   - Act in earnest
6. Sharing the Talk with the Audience
   - Talk in terms of your listeners' interests
   - Give honest, sincere appreciation
   - Identify yourself with the audience
   - Make your audience a partner in your talk
   - Play yourself down

The Purpose of Prepared and Impromptu Talks

7. Making the Short Talk to Get Action
   - Give your example, an incident from your life

- State your point, what you want the audience to do
- Give the reason or benefit the audience may expect

8. Making the Talk to Inform

- Restrict your subject to fit the time at your disposal
- Arrange your ideas in sequence
- Enumerate your points as you make them
- Compare the strange with the familiar
- Use visual aids

9. Making the Talk to Convince

- Win confidence by deserving it
- Get a Yes-response
- Speaking with contagious enthusiasm
- Show respect and affection for your audience
- Begin in a friendly way

10. Making Impromptu Talks

- Practice impromptu speaking
- Be mentally ready to speak impromptu
- Get into an example immediately
- Speak with animation and force
- Use the principle of the Here and the Now
- Don't talk impromptu—Give an impromptu talk

The Art of Communicating

11. Delivering the Talk

- Crash through your shell of self-consciousness
- Don't try to imitate others—Be yourself

- Converse with your audience
- Put your heart into your speaking
- Practice making your voice strong and flexible

The Challenge of Effective Speaking

12. Introducing Speakers, Presenting and Accepting Awards
    - Thoroughly prepare what you are going to say
    - Be enthusiastic
    - Thoroughly prepare the talk of presentation
    - Express your sincere feelings in the talk of acceptance
13. Organising the Longer Talk
    - Get attention immediately
    - Avoid getting unfavourable attention
    - Support your main ideas
    - Appeal for action
14. Applying What You Have Learned
    - Use specific detail in everyday conversation
    - Use effective speaking techniques in your job
    - Seek Opportunities to speak in public
    - You must persist
    - Keep the certainty of reward before you

Don't Grow Old — Grow Up!

The first step towards maturity — Responsibility

1. Don't kick the Chair. Be willing to account for yourself; don't blame others.

2. Damn the Handicaps! - Full Speed Ahead. Don't make a handicap an excuse for failure.
3. Five Ways to Ditch Disaster:
   - Accept the inevitable; give time a chance.
   - Take action against trouble.
   - Concentrate on helping others.
   - Use all of life while you have it.
   - Count your blessings.

Action is for adults

1. Belief is the Basis for Action. Know what you believe and act accordingly.
2. Analyse Before You Act.
3. Two Wonderful Words that Changed a Life. When the time for action arrives, don't hesitate.

Three great rules for mental health: Know yourself, Like yourself, Be yourself

1. There's Only One Like You Learn to Know Yourself by:
   - Cultivating moments of solitude.
   - Breaking through the habit barrier.
   - Developing excitement and enthusiasm.
2. Conformity: Refuge of the Frightened — Be yourself by developing your own convictions and standards; then have the courage to live with them.
3. Why is a Bore? Develop inner resources to avoid boring yourself and others.
4. The Maturing Mind: Adventure in Adult Living. Develop your mind through intellectual activity.

Marriage is for grownups

1. How to Get Along with Women. Here are seven ways:
   - Give her appreciation.
   - Be generous and considerate.
   - Keep yourself attractive.
   - Understand a woman's work.
   - Be dependable.
   - Share her interests.
   - Love her.
2. Father Come Home. Children need fathers too.
3. How to Get Along with Men. Here are seven ways:
   - Be good-natured.
   - Be a good companion.
   - Be a good listener.
   - Be adaptable.
   - Be efficient, not officious.
   - Be glad you're a woman.
4. The Rediscovery of Love. We must develop a more mature concept of love.

Maturity and making friends

1. Loneliness: The Great American Disease.
2. People are Wonderful. Learn to appreciate them.
3. Why Should People Like You? They will like you if you like them and develop qualities of warmth that attract others.

How old are you?

1. If You're Afraid of Growing Old, Read This. Learn some of the facts about aging.
2. How to Live to be 100 and Like it. To live longer, develop attitudes that promote health of mind.
3. Don't Let the Rocking Chair Get You. Work as long as you can.

Maturity of spirit

1. The Court of Last Appeal. When all else fails, try God.
2. The Food of the Spirit. Our spirit is nourished through prayer.

■■■

Chapter 3

Interpersonal and Communication Skills

"Interpersonal skills" refers to mental and communicative algorithms applied during social communications and interactions in order to reach certain effects or results. The term "interpersonal skills" is used often in business contexts to refer to the measure of a person's ability to operate within business organisations through social communication and interactions. Interpersonal skills are how people relate to one another.

As an illustration, it is generally understood that communicating respect for other people or professionals within the workplace will enable one to reduce conflict and increase participation or assistance in obtaining information or completing tasks.

For instance, in order to interrupt someone who is currently preoccupied with a task in order to obtain information needed immediately, it is recommended that a professional utilise a deferential approach with language such as, "Excuse me, are you busy? I have an urgent matter to discuss with you if you have the time at the moment." This allows the receiving professional to make their own judgement regarding the importance of their current task versus entering into a discussion with their colleague.

While it is generally understood that interrupting someone with an "urgent" request will often take priority, allowing the receiver of the message to judge independently the request and agree to further interaction will likely result in a higher quality interaction. Following these kinds of heuristics to achieve better professional results generally results in a professional being ranked as one with 'good interpersonal skills.' Often these evaluations occur in formal and informal settings.

Having positive interpersonal skills increases the productivity in the organisation since the number of conflicts is reduced. In informal situations, it allows communication to be easy and comfortable.

People with good interpersonal skills can generally control the feelings that emerge in difficult situations and respond appropriately, instead of being overwhelmed by emotion.

The ability to communicate is the primary factor that distinguishes human beings from animals. And it is the ability to communicate well that distinguishes one individual from another.

The fact, is that apart from the basic necessities, one needs to be equipped with habits for good communication skills, as this is what will make them a happy and successful social being.

In order to develop these habits, one needs to first acknowledge the fact that they need to improve communication skills from time to time. They need to take stock of the way they interact and the direction in which their work and personal relations are going. The only constant in life is change, and the more one accepts one's strengths and works towards dealing with their shortcomings, especially in the area of communication skills, the better will be their interactions and the more their social popularity.

The dominating question that comes here is: How to improve communication skills? Well, the answer is simple. One can find plenty of literature on this. There are also experts, who conduct workshops and seminars based on communication skills of men and women.

In fact, a large number of companies are bringing in trainers to regularly conduct sessions on the subject, in order to help their workforce maintain better interpersonal work relations.

Today, effective communication skills have become a predominant factor even while recruiting employees. While interviewing candidates, most interviewers judge them on the basis of the way they communicate. They believe that skills can be improvised on the job; but ability to communicate well is important, as every employee becomes the representing face of the company.

Developing Interpersonal Skills

You may be accustomed to doing things on your own, but sometimes "two heads are better than one." Considering the ideas of co-workers, even if they are different from yours, leads to creative and effective approaches to solving problems and getting work done.

Employers appreciate employees who get along with

people at all levels; therefore, they seek employees who have good interpersonal skills, such as communication, problem solving, and teamwork abilities. Interpersonal skills enable you to work with others harmoniously and efficiently.

Working well with others involves understanding and appreciating individual differences. It also means using those differences to your best advantage

Developing Assertive Approaches

Being assertive involves stating your point clearly and positively. Developing an assertive approach is an important step in your evolution towards full self-expression. Ask yourself:

- Can I complain about an unreasonable workload?
- Can I ask questions and make statements without fear of sounding stupid or incompetent?
- Can I stand up for my rights when a friend or a co-worker is rude or unreasonable?

When developing an assertive approach, first think of how you would like to be treated. Most people respect someone who is honest and direct, but you should be respectful of others rights and feelings as well as your own. By showing respect for your own feelings and those of others, you can achieve your desired goals. When assertiveness is practiced at work, everyone wins.

Accepting Responsibilities

Accepting responsibilities that go along with your career can help you to advance in your profession. The responsibilities you will be facing at work consist of:

- responsibilities that come with the job,
- responsibilities that you voluntarily assume, and
- responsibilities that arise from a situation.

Usual Work Responsibilities

Your everyday work responsibilities should be clearly described to you upon being hired. These responsibilities will vary from career to career; however, overall they consist of tasks that get work completed and objectives met for the employer.

Your entry-level position may cover a wide range of duties, so if you are asked to perform a duty that is not in your job description, check with a mentor or friend. It is better to say refuse to do the work than to repeatedly perform poorly or to complete a task that is someone else's responsibility.

- If you are not sure how a duty should be performed, always ask for clarification.
- If you make an error, take ownership for the error; it is a sign of growth and maturity.
- If someone corrects your error, you should show appreciation and not feel threatened.

Additional Responsibilities

Accepting additional responsibilities can be done voluntarily or involuntarily. In most realistic work situations, you will be asked to accept responsibilities that are not included in your job description. Handling these requests in a positive and assertive manner can lead to career success.

By taking on additional responsibilities, you can

- learn new skills,
- improve your chances for advancement,

- make a positive contribution to the department and company,
- assist a co-worker, and
- help meet deadlines.

New skills and additional responsibilities can always be added to your resume, thus making you more employable.

Resolving Conflicts

Conflict occurs in situations in which there is opposition. Opposition occurs when a solution cannot be found in a disagreement. Conflict resolution involves identifying areas of agreement and areas of compromise so that a solution to the disagreement or conflict occurs.

Many causes of conflict arise due to miscommunication. In these situations, your assertiveness skills are of special need. For example, active listening will help you to hear the real message. Sometimes you hear the wrong message due to one or more of the following factors:

- Cultural differences
- Differences of opinion
- Unclear roles or expectations
- Emotional responses to an issue or person
- Unequal status
- Misunderstanding of the language

Becoming aware of these barriers to effective listening can allow you to work towards focussing on the message and the intention, rather than on distracters.

There are five methods to handle conflict:

- Running away
- Being obliging to the other party
- Defeating the other party
- Winning a little/ losing a little
- Co-operating

Working in Teams

The amount of work to be accomplished in today's work environments has increased about as fast as the technological advances have permitted. Since the work to be done is often complex, requiring the expertise of several individuals, teams are formed to meet deadlines, project requirements, and budgets.

Employers greatly value individuals who can work effectively in teams because they can

- contribute efficiently to the organisation's goals,
- complete complex projects rapidly, and
- respect other team members' thoughts and opinions.

Listen to what people have to say, and help them in any way you can. Communicate ideas at staff meetings even if you have not fully thought the ideas through.

You may be surprised that with the ideas and creativity of your co-workers, your idea can be brought to fruition. Consequently, you may be asked to lead a team project; don't hesitate to take charge when appropriate.

Ways to Improve Your Interpersonal Skills

Don't discount the importance of interpersonal skills in the workplace. How you are perceived by your manager and coworkers plays a large role in things as minor as your day-to-day happiness at the office and as major as the future of your career.

No matter how hard you work or how many brilliant ideas you may have, if you can't connect with the people who work around you, your professional life will suffer. The good news is that there are several concrete things that you can do to improve your social skills and become closer to your colleagues. All of these tools will ultimately help you succeed in today's working world.

Try these Ten helpful tips for improving your interpersonal skills:

- **Smile.** Few people want to be around someone who is always down in the dumps. Do your best to be friendly and upbeat with your co-workers. Maintain a positive, cheerful attitude about work and about life. Smile often. The positive energy you radiate will draw others to you.
- **Be appreciative.** Find one positive thing about everyone you work with and let them hear it. Be generous with praise and kind words of encouragement. Say thank you when someone helps you. Make colleagues feel welcome when they call or stop by your office. If you let others know that they are appreciated, they'll want to give you their best
- **Pay attention to others.** Observe what's going on in other people's lives. Acknowledge their happy milestones, and express concern and sympathy for difficult situations such as an illness or death.

  Make eye contact and address people by their first names. Ask others for their opinions.

- **Practice active listening.** To actively listen is to demonstrate that you intend to hear and understand another's point of view. It means restating, in your own words, what the other person has said.

  In this way, you know that you understood their meaning and they know that your responses are more than lip service. Your co-workers will appreciate knowing that you really do listen to what they have to say.

- **Bring people together.** Create an environment that encourages others to work together. Treat everyone equally, and don't play favourites.

  Avoid talking about others behind their backs. Follow up on other people's suggestions or requests. When you make a statement or announcement, check to see that you have been understood. If folks see you as someone solid and fair, they will grow to trust you.

- **Resolve conflicts.** Take a step beyond simply bringing people together, and become someone who resolves conflicts when they arise. Learn how to be an effective mediator. If co-workers bicker over personal or professional disagreements, arrange to sit down with both parties and help sort out their differences.

  By taking on such a leadership role, you will garner respect and admiration from those around you.

- **Communicate clearly.** Pay close attention to both what you say and how you say it. A clear and effective communicator avoids misunderstandings with co-workers, colleagues, and associates.

  Verbal eloquence projects an image of intelligence and maturity, no matter what your age. If you tend to blurt out anything that comes to mind, people won't put much weight on your words or opinions.

- **Humour them.** Don't be afraid to be funny or clever. Most people are drawn to a person that can make them laugh. Use your sense of humour as an effective tool to lower barriers and gain people's affection.
- **See it from their side.** Empathy means being able to put yourself in someone else's shoes and understand how they feel. Try to view situations and responses from another person's perspective.

  This can be accomplished through staying in touch with your own emotions; those who are cut off from their own feelings are often unable to empathise with others.
- **Don't complain.** There is nothing worse than a chronic complainer or whiner. If you simpl y have to vent about something, save it for your diary. If you must verbalise your grievances, vent to your personal friends and family, and keep it short. Spare those around you, or else you'll get a bad reputation.

Communication Skills

Communication has been the major ingredient for the upgradation of the apes into human beings. Before language and the science of semantics were developed, facial expressions and body movements were the most sought after means for communication.

Slowly the language started shaping up and now we have countless thousand dialects.

Language is a medium that binds all human beings. It is the unique form, which has been exploited and used to the maximum by us. But somewhere down the line, we used it only for the purpose of communication and not for enriching our knowledge and to increase our market value.

You would be thinking what I am getting at? In the following few lines, I will clear all the question marks in your head. Tell me the number of times you have been engrossed in a talk or lecture given by someone? May be once or twice or maximum thrice.

Now the point to ponder is what was the distinguishing feature of that cogent speaker that didn't make your eyelids heavy with sleep? He would have had the knack to maneuver all your thinking, listening and visual channels towards him.

Closer observation would reveal that change of tone at the appropriate time, fluency in language, and proper translation of thoughts into words make his speech all the more appealing. He is able to give you what you want to hear and what he wanted to give the audience in terms of knowledge.

And when this success ratio is unity, you never skip a word from the speaker. Communication skills are an important forte and they add a very important dimension to your personality.

When you communicate clearly and openly, you always make your wants, needs and doubts obvious. This clarity is essential to market yourself and synchronises yourself with other two-legged intellectuals like you.

You may not be that well qualified, but with good communication skills you can crack your interview and you can sell yourself convincingly. You then don't try to fill in a vacancy in a company but make a place for yourself.

Some of the essential tips for communication include:

- Be clear, concise and straightforward.
- Keep your sentences short. This will avoid grammatical mistakes.
- Look into the eyes of the person you are speaking to. This gives a glimpse of your sincerity and dedication to the other person.
- Even if you slip up somewhere, maintain your calm, apologise and continue. Don't try to reanalyse such slip ups, because we wish to promote ourselves and not demote.

Communion Demands

Talking is very easy, but communication, that means an exchange or communion with the other person, requires the greater skill. An exchange which is the communion demands on the way we listen and do speak skilfully, and just not talk mindlessly. Interacting with the fearful, angry or the frustrated people will be even more difficult, because we are less skilful when we are caught up in such kind of emotions. Do not despair or resign yourself to the lifetime of miscommunication at the work or at home! Good communicators can honed as well as born. Here are few of the tips to get you started.

This will remind us how difficult it is to communicate effectively in any of the organisation. The problem is not that we have got the bad people, the problem is that we have got the poor systems. This guide will teach how to overcome the communication barriers and also hone the communication skills.

The Communication is the skill and like any other skills it also requires the practice. It is improved through practice which differentiates the skill from other forms of the knowledge. Understanding a theory of the communication and the effective presentation will not make you brilliant communicator or the presenter but should make you aware of how to maximise a impact of the presentations.

Most important thing to remember is a message which you intend to communicate is most likely to be misunderstood by the listeners.

Therefore, in addition to the carefully preparing and presenting the message, stay alert for any of the signs which your audience is misinterpreting it. It is up to you, a presenter, to continually check if your message has been received, understood, interpreted correctly and is filed in the receivers mind.

Effective Communication Fundamentals

Communication is the complex two-way process, involving encoding, translation and the decoding of the messages. The effective communication requires a communicator to translate their messages in the way which is specifically designed for the intended audience.

Creating and delivering the effective presentation requires basic understanding of a communication process. Most of the business presentations require a clear and an unambiguous communication of the message in the way which can be clearly understood by a recipient.

Tips for Effective Communication

- Be honest while communicating. Dishonesty will somewhere show up along a line.
- Take interest in the people you are communicating with.

Remember the people are more attracted towards those who have interest in them, and pays more attention to what they say.

- Think before you speak or put pen to paper: what message you trying to convey? What outcome do you want to elicit?
- Be direct and not aggressive. Lot of flannelling around can make the people lose interest and miss a vital point.
- Don't use the jargon – and acronyms, and also the technical expressions, unless you are sure about that your listeners do understand.
- Write the way as you will speak. Do not fall into a trap of using the long words just because it is written down.
- Take time. Whether in the speech or in paper, rushing will make you seem nervous, unconfident and like downright scared.

Techniques of Self-improvement

The term self-improvement refers to self-guided improvement—economically, intellectually, or emotionally—often with a substantial psychological basis.

Self-improvement often takes place on the basis of self-reliance, of publicly available information, or of support groups where people in similar situations join together. From early exemplars in self-driven legal practice and home-spun advice, the connotations of the phrase have spread and often apply particularly to education, business, psychological or psychotherapeutic nostrums, purveyed through the popular genre of self-improvement books and through self-improvement personal-development movements. According to the *APA Dictionary of Psychology*, potential benefits of self-improvement groups that professionals may not be able to provide include friendship, emotional support, experiential knowledge, identity, meaningful roles, and a sense of belonging.

Groups associated with health conditions may consist of patients and/or their careers. As well as featuring long-time members sharing experiences, these health groups can become lobby groups and clearing-houses for educational material. Those who help themselves by learning about health problems do exemplify self-improvement, while one might better regard help in this context as peer-to-peer support.

A Simple Self-improvement Technique

Self-improvement can turn into an enjoyable, rewarding and empowering activity. Look at the people around you and watch how they behave. If you find a trait of character or a certain behaviour, which you do not like, examine yourself closely and as impartially as possible, and find out whether you act or behave in the same way. If you do, then think and visualise how you would like to behave in a similar situation. Then, whenever you have the time, perform mental rehearsals of the new behaviour. Visualise yourself in the same situation, but acting in the way you want to behave.

Think often about the importance and advantages of a changed and more positive behaviour. Tell yourself again and again that you will remember to act differently the next time you are in a situation or circumstances that trigger the behaviour patterns that you want to change.

At the first attempts you will probably forget to act as desired, but keep visualising and thinking about the new behaviour patterns, and you will see how you gradually change.

Whenever you see people acting in a way that brings them

positive results, analyse what they are doing, their body language and the way they are talking and acting, and try to act and behave the same. If you keep doing so, you will soon start to see changes in yourself and in your life.

The advantage of this technique is that you can use it everywhere, anytime, without any prior preparations. Furthermore, this can turn in to a pleasurable game. You can use this technique while waiting for someone or something, while sitting on a bench in a park or while travelling in a bus or train. You can use your time more advantageously, instead of just letting the time pass by.

Two Examples of this Self-improvement Technique

You see one of your co-workers acting angrily. You watch his body language and the tone of his voice and see how people avoid him because of that. Now, look into yourself with an unbiased eye, and find out if you are guilty of the same kind of behaviour. If you are not, that's okay, but if you are, think about the consequences of this behaviour and the advantages of acting differently. Think how a calm and happy attitude can change your life and how people would treat you.

The next step is to visualise yourself in circumstances that trigger the kind of behaviour you wish to avoid, and to see yourself acting in a new and positive manner. Rehearse in your mind, in detail, how you would like to act, so that when you encounter this situation, your subconscious mind will guide you to act as you visualised.

Mentally rehearsing the new behaviour will remind you to act so in real life, and will also motivate and direct you to act accordingly.

Here is another example. You enter a shop and ask the

saleswoman some questions. She is patient, calm and answers all of your questions politely and with a smile. Her behaviour causes you to feel good and to like her, which may consequently make you to desire to buy something from her.

Analyse the behaviour of the saleswoman, and see what you can do to emulate her. Tell yourself over and over again that you too, are going to behave politely and patiently.

Visualise yourself in various situations that usually make you angry and impatient, and ask yourself why you behave in that way. Then start visualising yourself acting and talking in a calm, polite and patient manner in your day-to-day life.

It is important to understand that thinking and visualising just once is not enough. You need to do so over and over again every day, even several times a day, until you see results.

The above two examples are only meant to illustrate how to make use of this self-improvement technique. Maintain an open mind, open your eyes, desire to improve yourself, learn from others, affirm and visualise, and your life will begin to change.

Inner Changes Bring Outer Changes

The quality of your life depends to a large extent on the quality of your inner emotional and mental life. If you are lazy, worry too much and afraid to try new things, you stick to the same spot. If you are not afraid to change your thinking, your life will soon change accordingly.

Your habitual thoughts, and the content of your subconscious mind determine your behaviour and the way you act in the world.

When you change the way you feel and think, you

ultimately change your inner vision, actions and behaviour. This causes your outer life to change accordingly.

Let's now see a few examples!

If you are the worrying type, you are probably afraid of changes, and prefer to stick to the same kind of life you well know. You see other people who attain success, and though you wish you were successful too, you do nothing about it. In your mind you see yourself living exactly as you are living now, and find it hard to imagine different circumstances. It may never occur to you that you can visualise a different reality.

In this case your way of thinking limits you. You constantly see in your mind's eye the same daily reality, and consequently your conscious and subconscious minds stay programmed to experience and attract the same kind of reality.

Suppose you come to understand and realise that your outer reality is shaped to a great extent by your inner world. This realisation will cause you to aspire to a better life. You will start to envision the kind of life you want to live. If you keep thinking and visualising a different and better kind of life, soon these thoughts will sink into your subconscious mind and motivate, inspire and energise you to take action.

The new thoughts will cause new expectations, and change the way you view the outer world. The inner changes in you will gradually affect your outer life. Your behaviour, and the way you act will change. You will have more energy, ambition and inner strength. You will get over your fear of change, and be ready to take action to change and improve your life, in accordance with the changes inside you.

Self-acceptance: What Is It?

We hear so much about self-acceptance from people, who

study or teach personal growth methods. What is self-acceptance? Does it mean accepting your weaknesses or negative habits and doing nothing about them? Does this mean accepting your behaviour, attitude and life style, and doing nothing to change and improve? This can be an easy way to give in to laziness, and to having good excuses for leaving everything as it is.

This kind of self-acceptance might make you feel a little better and alleviate feelings of guilt, but it does not contribute to real progress and improvement.

The term self-acceptance seems not to be well explained and well understood. Accepting yourself as you are in only the first step. It helps you realise your good and not so good qualities, and can alleviate lack of self-esteem, lack of satisfaction and the sense of unhappiness.

Self-acceptance does not mean that you accept what you are and do nothing to change and improve. It does not mean accepting your fate and life as it is.

Becoming aware and acknowledging your behaviour, habits and your personality, and not being afraid to look at yourself as you are, is the first step to self-acceptance.

When you accept yourself as you are, you put yourself in a better position to begin improving yourself. It is not an excuse for saying, "This is what I am. I accept myself as I am. I accept my character, my failings and my fate, and this how it is. I can do nothing about it." Knowing yourself affords you the possibility to see what you can do to improve yourself and your life.

Improvement requires that you understand and acknowledge your character and habits, stop comparing yourself and your achievements to others, and acknowledging your skills or the lack of them. This will bring some sort of inner peace, lightness and happiness, like getting rid if a burden. This is the first step to self-acceptance.

Acknowledging your good and bad habits and traits of character can alleviate feelings of dissatisfaction, anger, resentment or unhappiness, but it is not an excuse for staying as you are, it is only the first step.

Getting Results from Self-improvement Techniques

Do you sometimes hear yourself or other people say: "I have tried positive thinking, and I have repeated affirmations, I have meditated and yet nothing happened"?

The fact is that few people use self-improvement or positive thinking techniques correctly, and fewer still do so earnestly and whole-heartedly.

You may start enthusiastically making affirmations for a few days, waiting for miracles, yet nothing spectacular happens. This makes you lose your enthusiasm and any confidence you had, and you disappointedly stop affirming.

You may start visualising something you want to accomplish or get, but when after a few days the object of your desire does not drop on your head from the sky, you lose your faith and stop visualising.

Maybe you have begun to meditate, but after a week or two saw no bright lights, neither experienced any altered state of consciousness. This made you conclude that meditation is just a waste of time.

Self-improvement and positive thinking methods work and

bring results, but only if they are used correctly. You cannot build a building, a bridge or an airplane, without the proper knowledge, training and preparation, and following instructions and rules. Self-improvement and positive thinking methods should be approached in the same manner. You need to know how to use these techniques.

It is not enough to say for a few moments, "I am achieving my goal, I am happy, I have money", and then revert to negative thinking and worrying. There is no magic in repeating a few words for a few moments.

How can you expect to accomplish anything by visualising, and at the same time worrying and having doubts about your ability to get what you are visualising?

How can you get any positive results if you sit for meditation, but instead of meditating you think about all kinds of irrelevant matters?

Success comes only if you fully and whole-heartedly desire what you are affirming or visualising and concentrate on the task. In order to see results you have to show interest and earnestness and do your best. Your inner vision should be strong enough to propel you forward, no matter how negative your current situation is, and despite any failures you may experience.

If you think, visualise, affirm or meditate for a few minutes, and then for the rest of the day think negatively, you neutralise or destroy all your positive thoughts, mental images and affirmations.

Self-improvement techniques and positive thinking work and bring results, if you are determined to succeed, follow the instructions correctly, persevere and do not let lack of faith, laziness and procrastination stand in your way. You need to give these methods time to work.

If you practice them as an unpleasant task, with no attention and concentration, how do you expect them to work? Be willing to devote time, energy and effort, where and when necessary. Success in self-improvement and positive thinking methods requires that you become involved, motivated and be willing to give them enough time to bring results.

Sometimes things happen in such a way that you could label them as miracles, but most of the time things happen in a more natural and gradual way. Inner changes will start to manifest, and will lead to outer change. Doors will open, people will help, circumstances and situations will change, and new constructive ideas will come up, all of which will bring the desired changes and improvements.

■■■

CHAPTER 4

Different Types of Personalities

Well-known behavioural scientists and psychologists have identified many types of personalities. We shall concentrate on the nine types of personalities. These are perfectionists, Helpers, Romantics, Achievers, Asserters, Questioners, Adventures, Observers and Peacemakers. They have their own unique personality traits that are briefly analysed below.

The Perfectionist

Perfectionists are realistic, conscientious and principled. They strived to live up to their high ideals. They can be got along well with if you take your share of the responsibilities so they do not end up with all the work.

You need to acknowledge their achievements. It is better if you tell perfectionist that you value his\her advice. Perfectionists also expect others to be fair and considerate, as they are.

A perfectionist would like to be self-disciplined and be able to accomplish a great deal. He would like to work hard to make the world a better place, having high standards and ethics.

They are reasonable, responsible, and dedicated in everything they do.

Example: The great Indian software business leader Narayan Murthy falls in the category of a perfectionist.

The Helper

Helpers are warm, concerned, nurturing, and sensitive to other people's need. That cab be got along well with if you tell then you appreciate them. They would expect you to share fun time with them. They would like you to take interest in their problems; through they will probably try to focus on yours. They want you to know that they are important and special to you.

A helper likes to be able to relate easily to people and make their live better. They are generous, caring and warm. They are sensitive to and perspective others feelings. They are fun-loving and generally possess a good sense of humour.

Example: Mother Teresa is one such personality who was sensitive not only to the needs of few people around, but for the millions of poor in the country.

The Achiever

Achievers are energetic, optimistic, self-assured, and goal-oriented. An achiever gets along well with his coworkers. He welcomes honest, but not unduly critical or judgment harmonious and peaceful. You cannot burden with negative emotions. He likes being optimistic, friendly and upbeat, and likes to provide will for his family. He is happy if he stays informed, knowing what's going on.

Achievers face problems when they have to put up with inefficiency and incompetence. They are gripped with the fear of failure or of not being seen as successful. They keep on struggling to hag on to their success.

Example: Sachin Tendulkar the greatest batsman, and Kapil Dev, the greatest all rounder, fall in the category of achiever-always full of energy to achieve something big.

The Romantic

Romantics have sensitive feelings and are warm and perceptive.

A romantic would like to get plenty of compliments. They mean a lot to them. He expects you to be a supportive friend or partner. If you care for him you respect him for his special gifts of intuition and vision. He would like to establish warm connections with people, admire what is noble, truthful, and beautiful in life; he would like to be creative, intuitive, and have a sense of humour. He is unique and is seen as unique by others.

Example: The great Indian painter MF Hussain falls in the type of romantic personality. He has a sensitive and heart and romantic personality for his creativity.

The Observer

Observers have a need for knowledge and are introverted curious, analytical, and insightful.

An observer likes to be independent, not clingy. He prefers to speak in a straightforward and brief manner. He desires and needs time alone to process his feelings and thought and may doubt your sincerity if you intensely welcome him. He dislikes intrusions in his privacy. He remains calm in a crisis.

An observer faces a problem which he/she is not sure of the situation and is unable to understand the relation between cause and effect. He gets disturbed if his integrity is doubted.

Example: The great economist Noble laureate Amartya Sen is one such observer personality, who is curious analytical insightful.

The Questioner

Questioners are responsible and trustworthy. They value loyalty to family, friends, groups and causes. Their personality rage broadly, from reserved and times to outspoken.

A questioner likes to be direct and clear. He likes others to listen to him carefully. You are required to reassume him that 'everything is ok between us' and not judge him for his anxiety. He is committed and faithful to family and friends, responsible and hardworking compassionate towards others, direct and assertive.

Example: The out spoken Bollywood actress and former Rajya Sabha member Shabana Azmi, may fall in this category. She can raise relevant questions in all platforms.

The Adventurer

Adventurers are energetic, lively, and optimistic. They want to contribute to the world.

An adventurer likes to get companionship, affection and freedom. He likes engaging you in stimulation conversation and laughter and expects you to appreciate his grand visions and listen to his stories. He is optimistic and do not let life's troubles get him down. He is spontaneous and free-spirited.

Example: The energetic NRI businessman, Vijay Mallaya, may be categorized in the adventurer type of trying something new that was not done by any Indian earlier.

The Asserter

Asserters are direct, self-reliant, self-confident and protective.

An asserter likes to stand up for you and is confident, strong and direct. He is vulnerable and shares his feelings and at the same time acknowledges your tender, vulnerable side. He likes to get space to be alone, He is curious to hear about his own contributions, but do not flatter him. He likes being independent and self-reliant, able to take charge and meet challenges head on. He is courageous, straightforward, honest, supporting empowering and protective of those close to him.

Example: The former Chief Election Commissioner T.N. Seshan, the straightforward bold officer, is the best Indian example of an asserter.

The Peacemaker

Peacemakers are receptive, good-natured and supportive. They seek union with others and the world around them.

A peacemaker does not like expectations or pressure. If you want him to do something, how you ask is important. He likes to listen and be of service, but do not take advantage of this. He us very easy to deal with if given time to finish things and make decisions. He likes a good discussion but not a confrontation. He is very caring and concerned about others, He is a good mediator and facilitator; he heightened awareness of sensations, aesthetics, is non judgmental and accepting.

Example: The former Indian Prime Minister Atal Bhihari Vajpayee has the peace maker type of personality.

Know Your Personality

Most people mistakes physical attributes of an individual as his/her personality. They talk about a marvelous personality when they may just he referring to an individual's stature fair complexion or chiseled features.

Well, if you thought that personality has anything to do with height, good looks, complexion or the physique of a person. It is time you re-think what you think you know. Any physical shortcomings can hardly influence of his personality traits such as superior character and behavior, and not by other mundane and frivolous considerations.

As per modern management concept, "personality is the BRAND IMAGE of an individual."

It is simple made up of three broad aspects namely:

1. Character
2. Behavioural traits
3. Attitude

Personality development is the improvement of behavioural traits such as communication skills, interpersonal relationships, attitude towards life and restoring our ethics. Character is the prerequisite to achieving a better individual personality. There are several behavioural scientists who argue that improving behavioural traits in a short-cut course of fifteen days to develop personality can effectively influence others and help win the race. But we must never forget that excellent behavioural traits such as communication skills, interpersonal relationships, higher order of motivational levels and excellent leadership qualities also fail miserably at the time of crisis if not based on solid character foundation.

Behaviour is just the showcase of the larger inventory inside a person, i.e. character. If personality is developed on the solid based of values and ethics, it will last forever. Fake smiles and mannerisms are short-lived and do not help in improving one's personality.

Good behaviour and co-operation makes a man popular.

As a result the possibilities of his progress and success increasingly multiply. The feeling of help and gratitude towards others not only adds to human qualities in a person but also increases his characteristic qualities.

Different people have different opinions about what makes a man's personality complete. There are several behavioural scientist who have the view point that character does not form a part of personality, but Steven Covey, one of the all—time great authors and motivators says that the best of behavioural traits fail if they are not based on the solid foundation of character.

The person who wants to improve his personality has to have *desire* and *determination*; he has to identify the *direction* for his goals to achieve it. Once all the above three steps are taken he has to dedicate himself to the task of achieving his goal. We need to develop personality traits that are very unique. Blindly following someone else who is successful will never take you in the direction right for you.

Components of Personality Development

There are immense possibilities within you to develop your personality with strong character. You must recognise and understand them. The key to success is hidden within you. The wealth you have earned is not important but what is important is the means you have adopted for acquiring that wealth. Your personality, your capabilities, your thoughts and your ideals are all very important in determining your character. We will discuss some essential components of personality Development in this article.

Be Polite and Speak Sweetly

Sweetly spoken words have their own advantage and it is a

major component in developing our personality. Society gives respect to a person who has control over his speech and everybody wants to conserve with a person who is sweet spoken. That is why we should always try and inculcate sweet and soft spoken words in our speech.

All actions are controlled by tongue or speech. They originate from speech. So it is essential that speech is controlled by mind. A person who is not honest by speech is considered dishonest in all respects. The man who has not control over his speech can not be sure if he can exercise any control over his self while working. If a wrong thing is said in good style it also becomes effective. Then if you say a good thing in good way it has no comparison.

Keep away from lies, Fraud and Deception

G.D. Broadman, a great western thinker said – sow a work and get a habit, sow a habit and get a character, sow a character and get a fortune.

It is evident that the fate of a person is formed by the work he dies, the branch of a tree bends in the direction it is diverted. If a person once entangles him self in lies and cunningness, then in spite of making countless efforts he can never get out of it and day by day he will keep moving toward downfall. We never improve our personality keeping these elements with in us or a part our habits.

Once a man resorts to lies for self-gains and self-protection then he gradually becomes an expert in telling lies. Lies, treachery, manipulation and fraud are such aspects of our personality which will lead to our failure, insult and defamation at every step of life. It is necessary that we get rid of these negative shortcomings with firm determination to get success in life. It is an admitted fact that bad ideas develop more rapidly as compared to good ideas. Therefore, we must try and keep ourselves away from all kinds of bad ideas and their impact.

Believe in Healthy Competition

The path of all success is filed with thorns. There is no hindrance in the path of downfall, but no sooner we lift the first step towards progress we start facing difficulties. Only those people who have immense courage and enthusiasm can advance on this path. Those who have moved forward have become immortal. These who cross all the barriers, all the pains, sufferings and sorrows are also able to taste the sweet fruits of success.

To achieve success it is necessary that all the energies of body, mind and wealth are utilized in one direction only. When a nab m avoiding all temptations in life works towards one definite foal, he is bound to get total victory. When all energies of mind and soul are concentrated for a particular work then all sources become available for completion of that particular work.

The Importance of Positive Attitude

Positive attitude is of great importance in our personality. Many people, inspite of having sufficient talent and qualification, do not progress and succeeds in life because of their narrow outlook. Nobody likes people who have narrow outlook. In life only that person is considered will behave who have positive and health bend of mind.

The real beauty of a man lies not in his physical appearance but in his work and good qualities. The ability and achievements of a person are judged by his mentality. That is why it is important that we improve our mental outlook. By adopting positive outlook we can get rid of mental dissatisfaction. This change will help you to contribute a lot in making your relations better and sweet with people as well as your personality will bright all over as like the stars in the sky.

Anger and Irritation are Your Enemies

To be angry is part of human nature. Probably there is no man in this world who has never been angry for some or the other reason. But some people are such who become temperamentally angry. People who get angry and irritated habitually do not realize that this habit of theirs will be a hindrance in path of their personality development and they will become their own enemies.

Anger results in foolishness and insanity. There is a saying that hot temper is the main obstacle in completion of delicate genes of the body. Sometimes delicate tissues and veins even get burnt, outwardly we do not come to know that damage has been caused but we destroy many hidden treasures in our body in fire of anger.

Spare Time for Social Service

If we want to be recognized in the society and want to reach the pinnacle of success, we should not keep out self-aloof from society. Our deep feelings and responsibility towards society makes us good and responsible citizen of the society we live in. The more we work for society and the more we remain connected with it, the more famous we will become the fame will enhance our personality and enthusiasm. Always remember that society is ours. We need it. Live not only for yourself but for the society.

Develop Your Creative Power

Our creative streak and positive propensity can pay us

dividends. One who is engaged in constructive activity of one or the other kind is always happy. All men should channelise their energies in creative work. Be it agriculture, physical labour, daily wager, craftsmanship, office work, domestic chores or social work. Breach in creativity is a breach in peace and happiness.

Know the Value of Time

Every moment of our life is a golden moment. The door of progress and development remain open for the person who knows to utilize and make best use of these moments. He not only pushes away all the failures and gets victory over all setbacks and obstacle but also becomes very popular in society dye to his punctual behavior. On the other hand worthless pursuits or pass these moments carelessly, face depression and disappointment on all sphere victims of vicious circle of failures.

Essential Personality Tips

Every man who wants to develop his personality also wants to become popular. Man's life is a burden without popularity. If we leave aside certain action, there is not much difference between a man and an animal.

Everybody can be popular if he/you takes care of these few enlisted personality development tips:

1. If you want to progress in life than honestly analyse the traits of your character.
2. Do not laugh at people when they are in difficulty or trouble other wise you will loose your personality in a moment.
3. This is a great way to develop your personality by listening

everyone politely, even if their ideas are baseless or not of your interest.

4. During conversation do not keep talking yourself too much.
5. When ever somebody brings any gift for you, don't forget to praise it. It does not matter even if you were expecting something else.
6. Make other feel that you love them.
7. Keep your moral high in case of defeat and be more polite on being victorious.
8. Solve your problems in a creative way. Try your best not to let these spoil your relations with your friends.
9. Enlist your bad habits and try to get rid of them.
10. We should not uplift our standard of living but also help others to do so. Try to remove the feeling of inferiority in others by loving them and by keeping good behaviour towards them.
11. Be careful of what your say about others because others will say the same thing about us at different times and at different places and in this way form a public opinion about us.
12. Some people often have a favourite sentence which they repeat frequently. We should try and get rid and get rid of such a habit.
13. Independence increases our good qualities and personality and slavery bad qualities.
14. Independent thinking and freedom to work is the only source of progress and welfare.
15. Love is the greatest magic in this world. You can do every

thing with help of love. Develop this art to improve your personality.

16. Positive attitude is of great importance in our personality. No body like people who have narrowed out look. In life only that person is considered well behaved who has positive and healthy bend of mind.
17. The real beauty of man lies not in his physical appearance but in his work and good qualities. That is why it is important that we improve mental outlook to develop our personality.
18. Every individual should develop the ability to adjust with others, because basically man is a social animal, so one can not survive by living alone.
19. Some people keep repeating a particular statement and it becomes a part of their nature. At the most you may repeat a statement twice but it you do it more than that it leaves a bad impact.

Ask Some Questions from Yourself.

1. Do you behave with your family members in the same manner as you behave with your master or your boss?
2. Would you like to joke even in such a situation when you that it would hurt the sentiments of other?
3. Do you take care of this that no one is hurt by you?
4. Do you take care of the feelings of those who are younger than you?

Project Your Personality through Good Behaviour

Man is considered superior and intelligent as compared to rest of the creatures. This is mainly because man is sentimental, and he has the capacity to express himself. Life is like a blooming flower. Sorrowful and gloomy people have not right to participate in celebration loving society. As far as possible our endeavor should be to create an atmosphere of love, happiness and laughter. We have no right to spoil the festive atmosphere by spreading tension and grief. Gloominess is such a fault/vice with not only isolated us develop and achieve the desired goals.

Life is the supreme gift of nature to man. We can know the real meaning of life of nature to man. We know the real meaning of life by making it useful for others. Life is full of

Both –sorrows and happiness—like shade and sunshine.

When one comes the other goes, but we should try and develop such an attitude that we may be able to lead a happy and balanced life under all circumstances. Keep one thing in mind that these worries and sorrows do not influence much your personality. The modern trends have changed life under all circumstances. The modern trends have changed life to a great extent. Today everybody seems to be stressed due to some or the other reason. But this does not mean that sorrows should overpower our personality and we should exhibit our sorrows everywhere. These work as shackles in the feet of any successful man.

For a well behaved person it is important to have good nature beside a pleasing personality. A good natured and jolly man, who is always smiling, attracts people towards him. The man who knows the interest of others and knows what type of conversation would please them and also knows to talk about appropriate things at appropriate time, certainly impresses everyone. Many a time in life we come across failures. A positives and hopeful attitude towards life helps us to overcome these failures and sorrows.

There is saying in English that "Thornless roses have not yet been invented". So people who wish to become beautiful and popular like a rose must learn the art of smiling and developing in life which is full of thorns as well. If we become dejected by our failures we should understand that we have learnt nothing from flower.

Flowers distribute their fragrance to everyone who enters the garden. They never express their grief. That is why whenever we come across a person with a smiling face we compare it with a blooming flower.

Sometimes our day may start with a bad news or bad information which may cause sorrow for us. This is also possible that the rest of the day may pass in despair. But we cannot keep pitying ourself for that. It would be unfair to do so . To get rid of the situation you can not wait for any other support. We have to make an effort to support our ownself from within. Whatever is happening within us and whatever is resulting with us, it is required that we concentrate on it and this can be considered a good beginning. Once when we become one with our inner experiences, we will be able to face all incidents, no matter if these incidents are unpleasant.

When we deeply practice this we realize that now we can honestly accept the facts of life as they come. Besides this, we are also able to observe the path which will indirectly lead to the solution of all problems and incidents.

When we are not in coordination with our soul, we invite lot many failures and lot many troubles. Purification of our own ability helps us to become more powerful. On the other hand if people feel that they have weak soul power they prove to be really weak –even if they don't agree to it.

The second emotion of gloominess is worry. Worry is

equivalent to funeral pyre. Worry brings many losses along with it, which adversely affect our heart, glands, nervous systems and complete health, Worries result in physical ailments. The strength and capability of a man decreases due to which his life becomes unhappy and troublesome. Worries decrease the life span of and individual. Worry is a process concerned with mental emotions. We can control worries by improving our thought process.

A scholar said that worry is the product of and idle mind. One, who does not like to work, likes to worry. If a man or woman is worried once people will come forward to help them but when they make it a practice then people start avoiding them.

There is an incident about Danial Bony, who was considered and eminent inventionist. When west America was being developed he faced many dangers in his life in spite of it he was blessed with 85 years of long life. When he was nearing the end of his life one of his friends went to meet him. He asked- "How did you manage to keep yourself safe from so many dangers?" Denial replied – "It was the will of God that I should develop and beautify this wild area."

Denial's life was full of troubles but his heart was full of enthusiasm. He believed that through his job was tough but it was useful, and that some Divine power is always saving him. It all of us can develop similar view point then we can get rid of unnecessary fears and worries.

Considering worry as something very harmful all psychologists advise us to keep ourselves free from it.

Worry is bigger than fire of death, worry is a bad thing, because fire burns a dead body whereas worry burns one alive.

Live of a person is just like a bubble of water in the river of life and when pain is beyond endurance it becomes medicine.

What is this pain? The desire, the eagerness to unite with God. In mortal world it is compared to unite with beloved. Here beloved is God and pain caused by His separation is suffering. And meditation acts as medicine to this state of pain and unconsciousness.

Boost Your Personality with Strong Character

The question of building a character is a personal matter for every individual. It has nothing to do with any other person. No other man can be instrumental in making you mentally and physically strong and powerful. None can turn you from weak to powerful, unsuccessful to successful and from nothing to everything. You yourself have the ability and potential of becoming everything and anything.

In today's materialistic world there is a rat race for achieving things at supersonic speed and there is chaos all around, everyone is involved in some or the other problem which does not seem to resolve. The sense of great dissatisfaction has set deep down to resolve. The sense of great dissatisfaction has set deep down in our hearts. We wish to board more money, more comforts and more and more luxuries as compared to other. This greed has overpowered us to such an extent that we do not hesitate in fulfilling our desires even at the cost of spoiling and ruining our relations with others. We are ready to do anything to make ourselves successful and capable. Nothing thinking and negative approach leads to downfall whereas the result of positive thinking, positive approach and good behavior is no less then a boon.

Today the progress/success of an individual is judged by

his materialistic achievements. Therefore, men adopt all fair and unfair means to attain materialistic components. It might be important to attain to lead a luxurious and comfortable life but this does not necessarily make you happy and successful. If we look around we can find many rich people and they did become luxuries of life but they had a miserable and they did becomes wealthy but they were unable to become good human beings.

People who are engaged in achieving materialistic things remain busy in developing only one aspect of their personality. The result is that their entire personality becomes imbalanced/ controversial.

Such people generally lack in striking a balance in totality, they lack farsightedness and tolerance. For achieving these qualities everyone should utilize every possible second of his/ her life. Any man, who wants to attain the highest pinnacle of success in his life, should meticulously work upon building a progressive and strong personality.

In the rapidly changing world and because of rise in new concepts each day new values/opportunities have appeared in the fields of industries and management too. People whose hearts are filled with human values, are blessed with special abilities and welcome new possibilities in life, there is ample scope of progress for them. It is evident that if most of the people working in any industry are able, experts and hard inspiring. For example, we can say that if the raw material is good then the product is also expected to be good quality.

Due to the difference in capacities of the people engaged in same size of units, the result is quite different. Uptill now it was believed that capital, raw material, and technical knowledge are the basis of success of any industry, but now it has become evident that we can progress in the field of automation with these things but we can not ignore human contribution in the organisation and smooth functioning in handwork, ability, behavioural excellence, enthusiasm and dedication of its people.

Excellence means not only to excel in achieving material gains but to achieve success in other fields of life as well and for this we must acquire such knowledge that may help us to achieve these aims in the best, quickest and easiest way. Excellence means to have complete control over our work hobbies, aims, habits, experiences and passions rather than become their slaves.

In other words excellence in personal behaviour also refers to growth/development of character. In his book 'Self help' Samuel! Ismail has termed character as the 'crown' and 'pride' of life. He believes that the qualities of character are those precious pears and respect in society. The qualities of character are even more powerful than wealth. According to John Gillen, "Excellence is an ideal quality. It is due to these qualities only that society recognized the importance of men."

There are immense possibilities within you develop your personality with strong character. You must recognise and understand them. The key to success is hidden within you. The wealth you have earned is not important but what is important is the means you have adopted for acquiring that wealth. Your personality, your capabilities, your thoughts and your ideals are all very important in determining your character.

Once a person went to a sculptor how would he make the statue? He was simply hammering a block of stone. The sculptor replied that statue can not be made, it has to be discovered by breaking the non-useful stone and once the task is done the statue emerges.

The seeds of great personality are hidden in every individual. There is not need to make them. You have just to unveil them. There is something that covers that goodness within us, we have to remove this cover. So do not ignore or neglect this precious wealth of character that eventually leads to development of your personality. There is a popular saying that generosity is the key to success. The secret of life lies in giving not taking. The more your give the more you receiving back with interest.

Amerson once said that the person who is always running after materialistic gains and comforts will always be found sleeping. To discover your own personality is greater than inner potentials existing within you is the best education in the world.

Saint Francis believed that it is because we give that we receive. A selfish/self centred man is least self dependent and most sorrowful. He depends on others for fulfilling his own selfish motives and therefore never achieves happiness.

Keep in Mind

- Our management and resources should be independent otherwise our ability will decrease.
- A person who believes in quick completion of his task may complete his task but he is never satisfied. He remains unsatisfied due to lack of enterprise and tendency of lingering on the work.
- Many of us would have achieved more in life if we had been honest enough to accept our mistakes and limitations.
- You can understand other people only if you love them and you have to pay its price by suffering some losses.

Sweeten Your Personality with Polite Speech

It costs nothing to be polite, but it definitely gives a lot. Its receivers become rich but the givers do not become poor. It is a relief for tired and ray of light for depressed, sunshine for the one facing cold and nature's best gift to the sufferer.

"I am highly impressed by you". This is a sentence which everyone likes to hear and feel honored. Your personality should be so pleasing and attractive that it should impress others, but it can not be achieved if you are not polite and soft spoken. The building of good qualities can only be constructed on the foundation of politeness. An ordinary man can become great if he is polite and if he is deprived of it he can lose respect.

Polite and cultured people are clear to all, such people have a strange magical touch in their conduct and behavior, and miracle in their deeds too. They cast permanent impression on the mind of everybody with their balanced behaviour.

Useful and sweet conversation is considered a blessing for speech. A man who dedicates his life for the cause of politeness treads on the path of truth, goodness and beauty, is like a saint.

There is an old saying that—'if speech is silver than silence is gold'. But in the modern age and fast changing world we have completely forgotten the meaning of this proverb. If we are in social field or we are at work place, we have to communicate with each other. In such situation we should take care of what is right and what is wrong. Many a times we spoil our work by unnecessary dialogue and conversation. We respect badly if we hear any adverse statement or if anyone teases us, we start hot discussion and fight if someone interrupts us. In this way we get involved in a vicious circle.

Think how nice it would be to listen to teasing remarks of

someone with a smile and keep ourselves busy in our work. To keep silence is a great art and a smile with silence is greater than that.

In this world there is enough to see and hear along with speaking. But most of us are so fond of talking that we fail to see and hear when we are engaged in talking. A person who can exercise control over his tongue, he alone can make the right use of his eyes and ears. It has been rightly said that after making any wrong statement due to its madness the tongue rests in the mouth but the cheek has to suffer a slap.

A little harsh conversation can result in hot discussion. It is generally observed that bitter and pinching words are the cause of dispute. The battle of Mahabharata is the historical proof of the disaster that Draupadi's one statement that 'the son of a blind man is also blind brought'. It is generally believed that the wound caused by an arrow can easily be healed but it is difficult to heal the wound caused by harsh words.

Society gives respect to a person who has control over his speech and everybody wants to converse with a person who is sweet spoken. That is why we should always try and inculcate sweet and soft spoken words in our speech. Generally a person suffers loss due to his uncontrolled speech more than anything else. Here the statement made in Mahabharata is noteworthy—"speech can also shower arrows and the one who receives them lives in constant pain day and night."

People who always talk about 'Frankness in speech' believe that if one does not give strong replies at once he is considered weak an inefficient. These type of people claim themselves to be pure hearted and frank. Psychologists infer such claims to be a sign of Pride. Pinching words can only be spoken if you have ill feeling against someone. Our speech is controlled by our thoughts. People who speak frankly without considering the pros and cons of their speech generally become unpopular and are not liked by anyone.

Anyone who always speaks the slump is disliked by others. If you analyses the things which you do not liked, most of them are those which are considered ordinary and are underestimated. In other words, we should take care of small things and the bigger things will take care of themselves.

Chaster Tan considers these small things as dangerously ordinary' and if not nipped in the bud, these will result into real troubles.

Sweetly spoken words have their own advantage in making a great personality. They tolerate the attack caused by bitter words and life becomes happy despite all kinds of troubles. In fact, these small sweet behavior is the outcome of feelings of love for others, It establishes this fact that all people want praise and recognition for their good behaviour, just as we do.

Bitter and uncontrolled speech is the symbol of foolishness. It can lead to madness. A person who often speaks harsh words often repents when he is in better frame of mind. According to a Persian proverb, "Good has given us who ears and one tongue so that we may listen more and speak less."

All actions are controlled by tongue or speech. They originate from speed. So, it is essential that speech is controlled by mind. A person who is not honest by speech is considered dishonest in all respects and this will adverse effect on your personality. The man who has no control over his speech can not be sure if he can exercise any control over his self while working.

If a working thing is said in good style it also becomes

effective. Then if you say a good thing is good way it has no comparison. Sant Kabir has said—"Speak in such a way that it may delight you and others as well"

Remember

To make your personality sweeten, remember when we have wisdom and the willingness to cast aside our own lower nature and align ourselves with our whole heart to the higher power, we find a sense of peace. This creates an atmosphere which influences every one who comes in contact with us. A person who has a peaceful heart, who is quite and self-controlled, cannot fail to radiate quietness and power which every one feels. We cannot be in contact with something that radiates blessing without conveying it to others, it never fails us. A high point of contact will redeem us and bless others.

Art of Facing Interview

The most commonly used tools for the selection process is the personal interview. An interview is a conversation with a purpose between two persons or groups of persons. They are done not only for the purpose of recruitment or selection for a post, but also to gather information from someone important.

Even through it is a two-way traffic, it is mostly seen that the employed is the one who asks questions and the interviewee is supposed to reply. Different purposes of a personal interview are – to rate a candidate for his physical appearance, education achievement and qualification, level of intelligence, background, interests and aptitude, There are different types of interviews, like:

1. **Informal Interview:** This is the type of interview that is conducted in an informal setting. The interview can be held at the residence of the managing director for the post of a

legal consultant. Similarly, many senior level job assignments are finalised during dinner at some hotel or restaurant.

2. **Formal Interview:** This is the interview that is conducted most commonly for recruitment of personnel. In such interviews the candidate is called for an interview at a particular location and time. The candidate is required to answer questions asked, based on the outcome of which he is rated for selection.
3. **Patterned Interview:** To maintain a uniform approach there are few interviews where a set pattern of questions are asked. In such patterned interview the choice of person conducting the interview is restricted and the selection criteria are also limited within a set frame.
4. **Depth Interview:** In such a interview, questions are based upon a specific area of the interviewee's interest. In a depth interview the person has to answer in detail. The academic competence and knowledge is tested thoroughly in such type of interviews.
5. **Stress Interview:** For the selection of supervisor and executive positions, it is of equal importance to judge the suitability of individual competence based on stress endurance along with knowledge and intelligence. Therefore a candidate is required to appear for the stress interview. In such and interview a person is required to respond to a tress situation and the assessment is done on the basis of the response.
6. **Group Interview:** When we are required to perform a task in a group the selection is done in a group interview and the candidate along with a group is asked to solve a particular problem. The performance and behaviour is, however, assessed and rated individually.

7. **Panel Interview:** For a senior level position selection, a panel of experts selects the candidate.

Personality and behavior traits are very important for performing well in interviews. Interviews, at times, become a hurdle between success and failure for persons just out of college. You have to present your competence for a particular job within a short period of fifteen to forty five minutes. The candidate is assessed for his behaviour, mannerism, attitude, IQ, stress enduring, capability, general awareness, knowledge of the subjects studied and mental frame of mind to take up the position for which he/she has applied. For a young student it is important that he prepares well for crossing this hurdle. He must be ready for the competitive written examinations as well as for the face to face interview.

Listed below are a few interviews do not and usual reasons for failure in interviews that every candidate should keep in mind:

- The candidate should not lack self-confidence or appear shaky.
- The hello-effect of the candidate should be impressive to the interviewing board.
- Poor communication skills are an absolute put-off.
- Body language must not reflect negativity.
- The candidate must not lack the relevant subject knowledge.
- There is a difference between self confidence and over confidence. Even if the expectation level of the candidate is high, he should not exhibit arrogance.
- The candidate's background and family history are important.

- The candidate must have reasonable amount of Knowledge about the company and the industry in which he has applied for employment.
- The candidate must not be improperly dressed or lack a sense of hygiene.
- If the interview board is harsh, the candidate must not lose his or her cool during the interview.
- The candidate must give a focused reply.
- Also, at time, the number of candidates is very large and board members are unable give sufficient time to each candidate for answering. Thus, answers should be as precise as possible.

Ten Simple Rules of Interview

Rule I-Behave as you are: A person facing an interview is generally nervous and does not behave as his or her normal self. He tries to follow the set guidelines that he has been told and in the process becomes very stiff and unnatural. Do not act, be yourself.

Rule II-Reach the interview site well before time: The early arrival at the interview venue will give you time to understand the office culture, the local etiquette and the expectation of the office and a chance to adapt to the particular environment. Reaching in advance also gives you the time to make yourself comfortable and more presentable by giving you time to freshen up. The settling time will help you to handle difficult situation properly.

Rule III -Try to know the company: The interview board expects you to know what the company is doing and what the industry norms the company is in are. Prepare from all sources such as the internet, company brouchers and other sources, if any. Try to find out the company's area of operation and expansion /diversification plans for which they are recruiting people.

Rule IV-Be focused: The purpose of your appearing for the interview is that you are looking for a job. The questions asked by the board will at times derail your prepared answers and will take you to a different direction. Try to be focused about your strength areas and the requirements of the company concerned. Try to be as short and straight as possible while dealing with a controversial issue.

Rule V-Behave as if you are already in the job: When a person applies for the job of a front desk manager, the interview board will like to see him in that pretext and would judge him keeping that person in the mould of a manager. If he starts feeling and behaving like a manager, half the work is done.

Rule VI-Be genuine and honest: Never lie to the board members. It is very easy for them to judge the truth or falsity of any statement or claim. Besides, everyone would like to reward your honesty.

Rule VII-Never answer question about which you are not sure: If you are honest in staying that you do not know the answer, people will appreciate it more than if you guess something absurd.

Rule VIII-Wish all members before and after the interview: It has been noticed that many candidates do not feel it necessary to wish the members and many others skip it due to nervousness. It does not give a good first impression of the candidate if he does not wish the board members.

Rule IX-Mind your body language: It is extremely important to mind your body language in the interview as you meticulously plan the words you utter.

Rule X-Anticipate the probable questions:

When we are to appear for an interview we do have a clue as to what questions the board will ask. Say, a person has an education gap of two years mentioned in his CV. The board would like to know what the candidate was doing during that period. Similarly, a housewife applying for a teacher's post will in all probability be asked about her routine for the day. Well-prepared answers for irritating questions will help you fare better in the interview.

Personality Test

There are several tests to judge the mental aptitude. Motivation level, attitude, inter personal skills and communications skills of a person. Many companies, prior to recruitment, conduct these tests as they find the formal way of face to face interviews not good enough to judge the personality of an individual. These personality tests are done in a controlled environment. The personality test can identify an individual's:

- value system,
- emotional reaction to a critical situation,
- moods and handling a crisis,
- ability to adjust himself to the stress of day-to-day executive lifestyle,
- self-confidence, personal ambition, emotional control and sociability etc.

To assess some of the behavioral traits such as impulsive,

emotional reaction, fear, patience, distrust, optimism, initiative and leadership capability, the companies generally conduct these tests. This can be used for the selection of the right candidate who can handle difficult situations with case.

There are three types of personality test, which are conducted by most of the companies. We may like to know what are intended for and how they are conducted.

Objective Test

These tests are conducted to assess the level of irrational tendencies in a person that arise in a not always get a working environment where all his subordinates are co-operative of his endeavour. These tests indicate the self-confidence of the person and also help in assessing the domination and submission of the person.

Projective Test

These are some of the tests in which a person is required to interpret the situation or react to a stimulus. The response of the person to these stimuli will indicate the person's motives, value and his personality in total. When we are required to react to such a situation, we always to interpret it in a way we deem is right as per our own value. The results will be biased if the person conducting the test has indicated his own view.

Situation Test

These assess a person's capability of handling stress. These tests are conducted in a room with no identified leader to guide it to structured discussions. The discussion is allowed to take its own course and people are allowed to come out freely and openly to express themselves. People generally behave spontaneously in such an environment.

Sisteen Primary Personality Traits

1. Reserved vs Outgoing
2. Less intelligent vs More intelligent
3. Affected by feeling vs Emotionally stable
4. Submissive vs Dominant
5. Serious vs Happy to Lucky
6. Expedient vs Conscientious
7. Timid vs Venturesome
8. Tough-minded vs Sensitive
9. Trusting vs Suspicious
10. Practical vs Imaginative
11. Forthright vs Shrewd
12. Self-assured vs Apprehansive
13. Conservative vs Experimenting
14. Group dependant vs Self-sufficient
15. Uncontrolled vs Controlled
16. Relaxed vs Tense

Traits for Buiding Positive Personality

1. **Accept Responsibility**

The price of grateness is the responsibility

– Winston Churchill

"Responsibility gravitates to the person who can shoulder them."

— Elbert Hubbard

Society is not destroyed by the activities of the rascals, but by the inactivity of good people.

2. **Show consideration**

   Show consideration, courtesy, politeness and caring.

3. **Think Win-Win**

4. **Choose your words carefully**

The principle is your speaking must be better than silent, rather be silent.

Words spoken out of bitterness can cause irreparable damage. The way the parents speak to their children in many instances shapes their children's destiny.

5. **Never Criticise, Complain and Condemn**

6. **Smile and Be Kind**

   Smile is the shortest distance between two people.

7. Put Positive interpretation on other people's behaviour:

We see the world not as it is, but as we are:

So when we are interpreting other peoples behaviour negatively we just reflecting our own mentality to this situation. In contrast when interpret positively, chances that other people may realise its negativity and change or amend this.

8. **Be a Good Listener**

Effective communication is 50% listening, 25% speaking, 15% reading and 10% writing. So when we listen carefully then 50% communication is done.

9. **Be Enthusiastic**

   Nothing great was ever achieved without enthusiasm

   — Ralph Waldo Emersion

10. **Give honest and Sincere Appreciation**

    The desire to feel important is one of the gratest craving in most of the human beings and it can be a great motivator. Honest and sincere appreciation makes one feel important and promote these positive qualities in him. In contrast giving false and insincere appreciation is flattery or sycophancy which in the long run is harmful to the receipient.

11. When you make a mistake, accept it and make it easy to amend

Mistakes are to be learned from. So accept it immediately and make change or amend easy.

12. Discuss but don't argue

Arguing is like fighting a losing battle. Even if one wins in the argument, the cost may be more than the worth of victory.

An Ignominious victory is a defeat itself.

13. Don't Gossip:

Gossip may lead to slander and defamation of character. People who listen to gossip are as guilty as those who do the gossiping.

14. Turn your promises into commitment

Commitment leads to enduring relationship through thick and thin. It shows in a person's personality and relationship.

15. Be grateful but do not expect gratitude

16. Be dependable and practice loyalty

An ounce of loyalty is worth more than a pound of cleverness.

Ability without dependability is of no worth.

17. Avoid bearing grudges

Life is too small to bear grudges.

John Kennedy once said "forgive the other person but don't forget their name."

Means "if one cheated me once it is his fault, but if cheats me twice then it is my fault."

Don't be cheated regularly to forgive.

18. Practice Honesty, Integrity and Sincerity

Lies may have speed, but the truth has endurance.

Honesty, Integrity and Sincerity have more enduring effect than the opposite.

19. Practice Humility

Confidence without humility is arrogance. Sincere Humility is the foundation of all virtues. It is a sign of greatness.

20. Be Understanding and Caring

The best way to be understood is to be understanding. And the basis of real communication is also understanding.

21. Practice courtesy on daily basis

22. Develop a Sense of Humour

Have a sense of humour and you will possess the ability to laugh at yourself. A sense of humour makes a person likeable and attractive. Some people are humour-impaired.

23. Don't be sarcastic and put others down.

24. To have a friend be a Friend.

Mutual trust and confidence are the foundation stones of all friendship.

25. Show Empathy

Empathy alone is a very important characteristic of positive personality. People with empathy ask themselves this question, "how would I feel if someone treated me that way?"

■■■

Chapter 5

How to Improve Your Personality?

Have you felt frustrated over a lack of success in your business and personal life? Do you secretly wish to overhaul your personality to help make these endeavours turn out more to your liking?

If so, don't fret. You are not alone. There are many people out there who feel the same way you do. And the good news is that you can discover how to improve your personality – starting today.

Whether you realise it or not, you already possess all the tools you need for a powerful personality — and total success in your life. You just need to use these tools to help bring about a brighter, better, truer you. So why haven't these tools been utilised yet? Fright, confusion, and mistaken notions about yourself have most likely prevented your personality from blossoming to its fullest potential.

It is important to remember that what you do is not the same thing as who you are.

You must discover the kind of person that you truly are.

Only by honestly facing that person, even if you do not like everything you see, can you develop a powerful and dynamic personality. It is this true and genuine self that people find attractive. They see through the mechanical and false persona that you are currently showing them, and they can't wait to discover the real you.

So how can you get in touch with the real you? It is quite simple.

The first step is to stop trying to please people. This doesn't mean that you should be rude and impolite to people. Rather, you should simply act the way you feel; be emotionally honest. Don't worry about what people think of you. Chances are they are not thinking about you nearly as much as you think they are.

When you feel frustrated, embarrassed, or angry, it is OK to let people see this. You are expressing your true feelings, and people will admire your ability to be open and honest.

Right now you might be thinking, "No one is going to like me if I act like this." Not true!

Ironically, people have the most respect for those who need them the least. An independent person gives off an inner power which others are very attracted to. By developing a casual attitude in your life, you will be a much more attractive person than if you are constantly trying to please others. This casualness demonstrates a lack of fear, which others will perceive as attractive.

So how can you develop this casual attitude that will attract those whose attention you are secretly dying to have? Simple. Follow these five basic steps:

1. Make a list of 12-15 people that you would like to attract.

2. Do nothing to attract them. Go about your life as if they are not a part of it.
3. If you hear from these people, be friendly and independent. If they ask what you have been doing, tell them you've been busy living.
4. Your relationship with these people is now on an even give-and-take level. Keep it this way. You can start giving back to them a little, but not more than they are giving to you.
5. Cross all those people off of your list that don't call on you. Their lack of effort to get in touch with you has demonstrated that your relationship is not mutual. Your goal in this process is to eliminate all one-sided relationships. These people are not worth your time.

As your new-founded relationships start developing mutually, it is OK to start taking more of an initiative in maintaining them. However, it is important to remember that if you don't see this initiative reciprocated, you should stop making the effort.

Over time, you will come to discover which people in your life are truly attracted to you and appreciate you for all of your great qualities. You will be surrounded by a strong group of sincere, caring friends before you know it.

Throughout this whole process, it is important to constantly work towards greater self-discovery. You need to drop the preconceived notions you have about what you are so that you can discover who you really are. If you are aware of the excuses and rationalisations you make for your behaviour, you can more easily start to correct these false beliefs about yourself.

As you become more self-aware and independent, you will

tap into your true-self and will see how to improve your personality naturally. You will be shocked to discover how much this will enrich your life.

Ways to Improve your Personality

Contrary to what you may believe, you can improve your personality.

The "personality" is the typical pattern of thinking, feeling, and behaviours that make a person unique.

When we say that someone has a "good personality" we mean that they are likeable, pleasant to be around, and good to socialise with.

Everyone wants to be attractive to others. Having a good personality helps – probably even more so than good looks.

While we can improve our looks to only a certain extent, we can work on improving the personality as much as we want.

Here are some ways in which we can accomplish this:

Be a better listener

Jacqueline Kennedy Onassis was considered one of the most charming women in the world because she cultivated the skill of being an exceptional listener. She would look a person in the eyes and hang on their every word.

Nothing is more appealing than having someone listening to you intently and making you feel like you're the only person in the world.

Read More and Expand Your Interests

The more you read and interests you have, the more interesting you are to others. It also gives you the opportunity to meet people and share or exchange your views with them.

Be a good conversationalist

This relates to how much you read and know. Once you have much to contribute, learn how to talk about it with others. We can't know everything, so it's refreshing to learn about things we don't have time to read about from others. If you're shy join a group like Toastmasters that encourages you to talk about what you know.

Have an Opinion

There's nothing more tiresome than trying to talk to someone who has no opinion on anything. A conversation has nowhere to go if you have nothing to expound on. When you have a differing opinion, it makes you that much more interesting and stimulating to be around (unless you're a know-it-all, of course). A unique outlook expands everyone's perspective.

Meet New People

Make the effort to meet new people especially those different from you. It not only exposes you to different cultures and alternate ways of doing things, it broadens your horizons.

Be yourself

The next most tiresome thing after having no opinions is to try and be something you're not. Trying to mold yourself to fit in and be accepted usually backfires. Everyone is unique and expressing that uniqueness is what makes us interesting. If we try to be a carbon copy of someone else, the lack of genuineness comes across.

Have a positive outlook and attitude

No one wants to be around people who are negative, complain a lot, or have nothing good to say. In fact, most of us run when we see them coming. Be the kind of upbeat person that lights up a room with your energy. You can do this by looking for the best in people and things.

Be fun and see the humorous side of life

We all like to be around someone who makes us laugh or smile. Look for the humorous or quirky side in situations. There always is one. When you are fun and light-hearted people are naturally attracted to you.

Be supportive of others

This is probably the most endearing quality you can integrate into your personality. Just as you welcome it when you receive it, be the support for others when they need it. Everyone wants a cheerleader, someone who encourages and believes in them, in their corner.

Have Integrity and treat people with respect

Be honest and true to your word and you will have the admiration and respect of others. Respect others and you will have their attention and gratitude. Nothing improves a person's personality more than integrity and respect – respect for others as well as respect for yourself.

As humans we have the power and ability to shape our personalities however we wish. When we strive to develop them to encompass all that we can be, we contribute to others and our own happiness.

Be an Interesting Person

In our culture today much emphasis is placed on looks, sex appeal and being youthful. Many individuals spend a disproportionate amount of time working on their outer packages. They go to great lengths to be fashionable and trendy as well as making sure they are seen at the latest "in" places.

Sadly, when little or no effort is being made to develop the intellect or an interesting personality, many good-looking young men and women come across as being flighty and uninformed, as well as self-centred and self-absorbed.

Evidence of this unhealthy trend can be witnessed in the behaviour of today's young celebrities and pop stars who often serve as role models (whether we like it or not) for our children. We are bombarded daily with news of their antics where they engage in self-indulgent and often irresponsible behaviour. Some of them end up in a re-hab which quite often doesn't address the real problem.

Although physical attraction is very helpful in the preservation of our species, evolution has come a long way in giving us more than solely our appearance to attract each other.

For a solid, meaningful relationship to develop between two parties they must have more to contribute to each other beyond their initial physical attraction.

When two people have little in common except for their good looks, there is virtually no place for a relationship to go. They must enjoy each other as individuals and be able to develop a bond or friendship. There must be substance, shared interests, willingness to grow, and mutual respect.

So what's the answer?

Become someone whose company others seek. Have something meaningful to contribute.

Become an interesting person by:

- Cultivating a variety of interests

- Taking a genuine interest in others
- Reading more
- Staying on top of current events
- Expressing your informed opinions

Develop all aspects of yourself – your mind, body, intellect and spirit.

It's never too late to start.

Dare to be an Original

When you dare to be an original you are in essence daring to be "yourself" and everything that encompasses who you really are. To many of us, that can be a scary and daunting proposition.

And why is that?

Because it means putting ourselves on the line. It means subjecting ourselves to scrutiny, judgement and possible ridicule. It means exposure and vulnerability.

Certainly there is more comfort to be found in conformity, lying low and blending in with the crowd.

There is also boredom, complacency and the prospect of never living to your potential.

It takes courage and self-confidence to dare to be an original, reveal your uniqueness or show that you're one of a kind. However, as with any frightening endeavour, the rewards of overcoming obstacles and prevailing far out weigh the consequences of not venturing forth.

As Steve Jobs noted in his speech at a Stanford University graduation commencement:

"Your time is limited; so don't waste it living someone else's life. Don't be trapped by dogma – which is living with the results of other people's thinking. Don't let the noise of others' opinions drown out your own inner voice. And most important, have the courage to follow your heart and intuition. They somehow already know what you truly want to become. Everything else is secondary."

It's true. Life is too short to live it trying to be anything other than your true, original self. Be who you are and be it the best way you know how. Celebrate your individuality and uniqueness. Dare to be an original!

Tips on how to be an original or your true-self:

- **Know who you are**

Before you can be yourself, you must know who that is and then be true to that self. Centuries ago Socrates wisely observed that self-knowledge is the pillar of all virtue. Without it nothing else is genuine.

- **Trust your intuition and instincts**

Part of knowing who you are trusting your intuition and instincts. We all have an inner gauge that guides us along our most fulfilling path. Look deep within to find the answers to your life. No one is better at knowing what you need and want from life than you. Of course, it's prudent to listen to the advice of family, friends and professionals, but you are the ultimate authority on you. You are unique and original and no one but you can make your decisions for you. To go against that intuition is to go against your fundamental nature and source of satisfaction.

- **Express yourself by cultivating your own style, tastes and personality**

Many people try to be like those who seem to be popular. Rather than work on developing themselves they try to copy others and lose themselves in the process. Much time is wasted in such pursuits and the results are disillusionment and feelings of failure.

When you work on cultivating your own style, tastes and personality, not only are you genuine and authentic, you're more interesting and attractive to others. Let go of fear and embrace your uniqueness.

Make your life an expression of who you are. As Steve Jobs said, have the courage to follow your heart. If you desire to be an artist, don't settle for being an accountant because your parents want you to be, or because you can make more money at it. In the end you will lose out because the money won't matter if you're unhappy, unmotivated or depressed.

- **Believe in yourself and don't worry about what others think**

When you choose the right path for yourself do not allow the opinions of others to distract you. People are good at offering well-intentioned, unsolicited opinions, however only you know what's best for you. Don't let a lack of self-confidence or self-doubt prevent you from pursuing what you know is best for you.

Let go of your personal insecurities. If you strive to be someone you're not, you will never be happy. Be yourself. Be proud of who you are. People who have a more positive view of themselves live better, healthier lives.

When you dare to be an original, you dare to be courageous, strong, and vibrant and are willing to realise the full potential of your unique skills and talents.

Benefits of being an original:

- You are true to yourself, therefore derive greater personal satisfaction and fulfilment.
- You are more noticed, interesting and attractive to others.
- You are willing to take risks, think originally and be creative, therefore are open to greater career opportunities and advancement.
- Due to a willingness to let go of convention, you live life to the fullest and on your terms.
- Whether in your career, the arts, or in your community, you offer a fresh, new, diverse perspective.
- You are usually a trailblazer, set new trends and discover new ways of doing things.

Be True to Yourself

To be true to yourself means to act in accordance with who you are and what you believe.

If you know and love yourself you will find it effortless to be true to yourself.

Just as you cannot love anyone else until you love yourself, you cannot be true to anyone else until you are true to yourself.

Be who you are.

Do not take action or pretend to be someone else for the sake of gaining acceptance.

Many young people believe that when they do things to please their peers, such as drink when they shouldn't, or behave and party in inappropriate ways, they will be popular and liked.

They go against the advice of their parents or their own

common sense only to find themselves in trouble and not accomplishing what they set out to do.

When you do things that are not genuine or a reflection of the real you, you will not be happy with yourself and will end up confused. You'll be confused because you won't know whom to please, or how.

Self-respect comes from being true to who you really are and from acting in accordance with your fundamental nature.

When you respect yourself, others will respect you. They will sense that you are strong and capable of standing up for yourself and your beliefs.

When you are true to yourself, you allow your individuality and uniqueness to shine through. You respect the opinions of others but do not conform to stereotypes or their expectations of you.

To be true to yourself takes courage. It requires you to be introspective, sincere, open-minded and fair.

Being true to yourself does not mean that you are inconsiderate or disrespectful of others.

It means that you will not let others define you or make decisions for you that you should make for yourself.

Know Yourself

To know yourself is your first priority

How can you set goals, go about life, and have relationships if you don't know who you are or what you want? You really can't.

To not know yourself leads to confusion and wasting much time in hit and miss situations.

We tend to underestimate the importance of knowing ourselves. Many of us go through each day reacting to events and just getting by rather than making conscious choices based on who we are and what we want.

When we don't know where we are headed it's hard to set goals, get motivated and determine the best course of action. Before we can do any of these things we must establish who we are.

To know yourself:

- Be aware of your strengths, weaknesses, likes and dislikes
- Observe and be aware of your moods, reactions and responses to what is happening around you
- Become aware of how these moods and emotions affect your state of mind
- Examine how you interact with others

Observe how your environment affects you.

Knowing and understanding yourself better, in turn, leads to better decision-making, setting and reaching appropriate goals and altogether living more productively.

On Self-worth and High Self-esteem

How to Build Self-confidence?

We, ourselves, have to build self-confidence and not depend on, or wait for anyone else's approval.

How we see ourselves is more important than how anyone else sees us.

If we don't work at loving and accepting ourselves, nothing anyone else thinks matters.

- **Acknowledge Your Uniqueness**

Believe in yourself and know that you are one of a kind. In the words of Walt Whitman know:

> "That you are here—that life exists, and identity;
>
> That the powerful play goes on, and you will contribute a verse."

There is no one else like you on this planet. No one looks like you, has the same talents, experiences or perspective as you do. You are unique and are therefore here to make your unique contribution.

If we each focus on what we bring into the world to share, there can be no comparisons, envy or regret. We are here to "contribute a verse".

- **Give it Your Best**

When you do the best you can, with the best of what you've got, you can't help but feel good about yourself and that confidence comes through in everything that you do.

- **Persevere**

Everybody has setbacks and obstacles to contend with. Don't let them undermine your confidence. Treat them as opportunities to strengthen your resolve and then persevere.

- **Overcome adversity**

Overcoming adversity builds and strengthens self-confidence. The greatest songs, works of art and literary pieces have been written by those who have experienced the depths of despair, loss and emptiness and overcame them. Experiencing sadness and loss and then rising above them gives rise to hope and triumph. It makes you stretch and become more than you were.

- **Accomplish something**

Set goals for yourself and then push yourself to reach them. Self-confidence soars when you know you can do what you put your mind to. It makes you feel unstoppable.

- **Separate Yourself From the Event**

You are not what happens to you or how you believe others see you. In other words, you are not defined by what happens to you or how others see you. You are who you choose to be a person of character, dignity and self-confidence.

- **Confront your fears**

There's nothing that destroys self-confidence more than succumbing to fear. Everyone feels fear at various times; we're human, however facing circumstances with courage and poise strengthens character and builds self-confidence.

- **Good looks do not equal self-confidence**

Some of the most attractive people in the world are insecure and lack self-confidence. Marilyn Monroe was considered to be one of the sexiest most beautiful people in the world yet she lacked a positive self-image.

She misguidedly allowed external factors to determine her self-worth. Good looks help you feel good about yourself, but are by no means enough.

- **Learn how to give yourself a pep talk**

We all have our down moments, moments of doubt, confusion and uncertainty. When that happens we have to learn how to restore our self-confidence. One way is to understand that everyone goes through such moments.

When that happens the thing to do is remember past

successes, visualise the desired outcome and keep at it. Practice makes perfect.

Self-confidence is absolutely essential to achieving success in any endeavor. You acquire it by doing, learning, accomplishing and persisting.

Self-confidence Action Plan: How to Start One?

While it is wonderful and absolutely necessary to possess personal confidence or self-confidence, is it possible to have too much?

Believe it or not, yes!

Even as most people lack enough confidence or possess a positive self-image, there are those who overestimate their capabilities, are over optimistic, take on too much risk and end up crashing and burning.

So why am I even bringing this up?

The answer is, because in order to build true/genuine self-confidence, your self-image must be founded in reality. You must know who you are.

You must have a realistic evaluation of your abilities and you must commit to continued self-improvement. Add to that learning to maintain focus, motivation and persistence, and you're on your way!

A good way to build and maintain your self-confidence and stay focused is to set up a programme or action plan for yourself. Here is an outline of how you can go about it. You can customise it to your own needs or you can follow the steps as I've presented them.

Self-confidence Action Plan

Become aware

Know who you are what you want. As has been said so many times – "If you don't know where you are going, how will you know when you get there?" Take the time to figure out what your strengths, aptitudes and capabilities are and how you can to best use them to achieve personal satisfaction and fulfillment.

Draw up a chart or excel spreadsheet outlining your strengths, what you enjoy doing, and how you can establish goals. List the things you'd like to do and what you have to do to accomplish them.

For example:

Strengths	Personal	Physical Abilities	Interests Abilities
reliable	good memory	coordinated	basketball
loyal	artistic	good stamina	play guitar
friendly	musical	quick reflexes	writing
trustworthy	good writer	good writer	computers

Some possible goals based on the above set of talents and capabilities might be:

- To stay physically fit by joining a local basketball league
- Start a blog on any one of interests to improve writing skills
- Join any network and develop speaking skills

If you don't take action or set goals, but just flail about aimlessly without purpose or focus, it won't take long before you become disillusioned and hopeless. Those who are self-confident know what they want and they work at getting it.

Motivate Yourself

Self-confidence comes also from the ability to motivate yourself to achieve your goals. Of course, it's easier to just procrastinate and find excuses for not putting in the effort to accomplish something.

Unfortunately, this too leads to inertia, disillusionment and falling into a rut. One way you can stay on track and stay motivated is to set up a chart of must-do activities that include:

- 30-40 minutes of exercise/jogging daily
- practice guitar for 30 minutes, 3 times a week
- write one article a week for blog
- read articles and newspapers for ideas and to sharpen language skills

Take Care of Yourself

Even though relying on your physical appearance and good looks as a basis for self-confidence is not a good idea, it *is* important to look and feel your best.

This means staying healthy and fit, maintaining good grooming habits and making the most of what you have. Do some research on the best styles and colours for your body type.

If you need help, there are many men's and women's fashion magazines that can give you some great ideas. The Internet is also a helpful resource for finding the latest trends and styles.

Pay attention, too, to your attitude. How you walk, talk, and conduct yourself significantly reflects how you feel about yourself. A good personality, a neat and stylish appearance and a smile on your face can take you a long way towards success in career, relationships and personal accomplishment.

Develop Your Mind

And then keep developing it! Not only will people find you interesting and someone who contributes to their own knowledge and awareness, you will keep your brain sharp and active.

People who get mentally lazy and don't continue to challenge themselves throughout life are more prone to develop dementia, Alzheimer's and other degenerative brain diseases as they age. Self-confidence will plummet!

Make it a point to do such things as:

- reading
- brain puzzles
- playing games such as chess
- staying informed of current events
- learning about global issues
- journaling
- memorise people's names
- improve your vocabulary

Stay on Top of Things and Reinforce

Continue to assess and evaluate yourself. Self-confidence can rise and fall depending on what you're doing with yourself. If you happen to slack off and choose not to keep improving, you will begin to feel uninspired and less confident.

Even the most successful people in the world cannot, and do not, rest on their laurels because personal growth is continuing processes.

Make sure, however that you do not to go overboard and put pressure on yourself to achieve. Learn to gauge yourself and balance striving to reach your goals with fun and recreation.

As you can see, self-confidence is not only an achievable goal if you set it up as a workable **Action Plan,** it can also be fun and extremely rewarding. Take the time to draw up your own self-confidence action plan and tailor it to your particular needs and goals where necessary.

Decide which characteristics you want to develop, work on or accentuate. Make a game of it. The process alone will stimulate your creativity and who knows what great things can come of it! Enjoy the ride as you become a more confident individual who is willing to take control of their own destiny.

Healthy Personal Boundaries and How to Establish Them?

Learning to set healthy personal boundaries is necessary for maintaining a positive self-concept or self-image. It is our way of communicating to others that we have self-respect, self-worth and will not allow others to define us.

Personal boundaries are the physical, emotional and mental limits we establish to protect ourselves from being manipulated, used or violated by others. They allow us to separate who we are and what we think and feel from the thoughts and feelings of others.

Their presence helps us express ourselves as the unique individuals we are, while we at the same time acknowledging the same in others.

Enjoying healthy relationships would be impossible without the existence of our personal boundaries and without our willingness to communicate directly and honestly what they are. This would include recognising that we are individuals with our own emotions, needs, attitudes and values. It would also mean acknowledging that spouses, children, friends and others are also separate individuals with their own emotions, needs, attitudes and values.

Setting personal boundaries means preserving your integrity, taking responsibility for who you are and having control of your life.

How do we establish healthy personal boundaries?

- **Know that you have a right to personal boundaries:** You not only have the right, but you must take responsibility for how you allow others to treat you. Your boundaries act as filters permitting what is acceptable in your life and what is not.

  If you don't have boundaries that protect and define you, as in a strong sense of identity, you tend to derive your sense of worth from others.

  To avoid this situation, set clear and decisive limits so that others will respect them, then be willing to do whatever it takes to enforce them. Interestingly, it's been shown that those who have weak boundaries themselves tend to violate the boundaries of others.

- **Recognise that other people's needs and feelings are not more important than your own:** Many women have traditionally thought that the needs of their husbands and children are more important than their own. This is not only untrue, but it can undermine the healthy functioning of the family dynamic.

If a woman is worn out mentally and physically from putting everyone else first, she not only destroys her own health, she in turn deprives her family of being fully engaged in their lives. Instead, she should encourage every family member to contribute to the whole as well as take care of himself or herself. Putting themselves last not is not something only women do, but many men as well.

- **Learn to say no:** Many of us are people pleasers and often put ourselves at a disadvantage by trying to accommodate everyone. We don't want to be selfish so we put our personal needs on the back burner and agree to do things that may not be beneficial to our well-being.

  The fact is, a certain amount of "selfishness" is necessary for having healthy personal boundaries. You don't do anyone any favours, least of all yourself, by trying to please others at your own expense.

- **Identify the actions and behaviours that you find unacceptable:** Let others know when they've crossed the line, acted inappropriately or disrespected you in any way. Likewise, don't be afraid to tell others when you need emotional and physical space in order to be who you really are without any pressure to be anything else.

  Know for yourself what actions you need to take if your wishes aren't respected.

- **Trust and believe in yourself:** You are the highest authority on you. You know yourself best. You know what you need, what you want and value.

Don't let anyone else make the decisions for you. Healthy boundaries allow you to respect your strengths, abilities and individuality as well as those of others.

Unhealthy imbalance can occur when you encourage neediness or are needy, want to be rescued/the rescuer or choose to play the victim.

Signs of Unhealthy Boundaries

- Going against personal values or rights in order to please others.
- Giving as much as you can for the sake of giving.
- Taking as much as you can for the sake of taking.
- Letting others define you.
- Expecting others to fill your needs automatically.
- Feeling bad or guilty when you say no.
- Not speaking up when you are treated poorly.
- Falling apart so someone can take care of you.
- Falling "in love" with someone you barely know or who reaches out to you.
- Accepting advances, touching and sex that you don't want.
- Touching a person without asking.

When we have healthy personal boundaries we are more in touch with reality, can deal with problems more easily and are better able to communicate with others. Having boundaries promotes a healthy self-concept, trust and stability and inspires better relationships. It's never too late to take the time to be aware of, or to establish healthy personal boundaries.

■■■

Chapter 6

Personal Effectiveness

Effective Goal Setting

The purpose of effective goal setting is to achieve what you want in life in a successful, focused and decisive manner by taking the right actions in a lesser time frame. Who doesn't want to achieve more in less time, yet many of us abandon our goals before we accomplish them?

Why is that?

Some of the reasons include: lack of confidence, not having a workable plan for achieving them, being unrealistic by expecting too much too soon, fear of failure and lastly by putting too much pressure on ourselves to accomplish them.

Luckily there are strategies and behaviours that can help us overcome the obstacles that get in the way of our setting goals and achieving them.

How do you Start?

Know that you deserve success and achievement

Before you can start setting goals, you must know that you

deserve success and that it is achievable (through goal setting) for anyone who puts their mind to it. You must believe that you can do what you set out to do, as well as in your talents and abilities. If you do not start with this crucial premise your efforts will be thwarted and you will fall short of accomplishing what you want.

Determine what you want

One of the biggest problems people have in trying to set goals is not knowing what they really want. If you are not clear about what you want in life, it's very difficult to get started. The one thing all successful people have in common is that they are intensely goal oriented and extremely focused.

They know what they want and they understand that it takes setting goals to achieve it. To get yourself going, a good idea would be to take the time to write down which goals are meaningful to you and what you would need to do accomplish them.

To help you figure this out, you can start by looking at the 'big picture' of your life. Start a journal or workbook and write down the answers to some important questions by asking yourself things like:

- Do I want to be in the best of health and what will it take to get there?
- What do I want to achieve in my career?
- What kind of family life do I want?
- What kind of lifestyle do I want today and in the future?
- How do I see myself in 5, 10 or 20 years from now?

For example, under a goal of maintaining good health, you might make a list that includes: exercising 3-4 times a week, eating a balanced diet of protein, fruits and vegetables, getting 7-8 hours of sleep etc.

Under where you want to be in 5 years you might include: finish college degree; be earning an income of x amount of rupees; have a serious personal relationship (or avoid having a serious relationship until career is established).

Plan, organise and prioritise your goals in smaller, manageable chunks

If you look at everything you want to achieve all at once, you might find it daunting and overwhelming so it's best to organise and prioritise your goals. To do so, you must devise a workable plan for each thing you want to accomplish. For instance, you know that your health goals need to be ongoing ones, so you could establish a daily routine or agenda that you'd want to keep up on a regular basis.

For a career goal, you could categorise it in monthly, quarterly or yearly chunks. You could lists points, or plan the actions you must take in order to get to a particular point in your career. This may include taking the odd supplemental course, doing extra reading or volunteering in the community to give exposure and experience in a certain field. Since careers take time and effort to build, planning and organising your moves makes good sense.

Review, update and revise

Review and update your goals on a regular basis to make sure they are still relevant to you. It's also important to make sure you are still on track and taking the appropriate steps and actions to get to where you need to be. If some of your actions aren't working, fine tune them or devise new ones. Likewise, figure out which obstacles and distractions are getting in your way and determine what you need to do to overcome them. We all know there are setbacks and bumps in the road along the way to achieving goals, but we need not let them stop us or take us off course. Revise and adjust the game plan where and when you need to.

Stay focused and motivated

Probably one of the hardest things to do in the process of attaining your goals is to stay focused and motivated. It's common to fall off the wagon every now then, however, it's essential to get back on as soon as possible.

One of the tools that can keep you focused is the journal or workbook you've been keeping. Go over it regularly as a reference point and to remind yourself what you want to accomplish. Set-up routines or habits that will ensure you stay on track, e.g. do your exercises at the same time each day; drink your protein shake first thing in the morning.

Other helpful techniques to help you stay motivated include the use of relevant affirmations and visualisation. Many successful people, especially athletes, swear by both techniques. You have to be able to see yourself as having achieved a goal before you actually do so. Likewise, positive affirmations help implant positive thoughts into your subconscious which prompt you to take the right actions to achieve your goals.

The Benefits of Setting Goals

- Gives you the 'big picture' direction you want your life to take
- Helps keep you organised and focused
- Builds self-confidence and a sense of accomplishment

- Helps you achieve success more efficiently and in less time
- Makes the small day to day tasks more meaningful and purposeful.

Goal setting has been a tried and true method for achieving success and accomplishing what we want in life. Without it we would drift aimlessly and waste valuable time and effort in pursuits that lead us nowhere. So start now and decide which goals are most meaningful to you and devise a plan to achieving them!

How to Think Positively?

What does it mean to think positively?

Quite often when we're going through a challenging time or we're just plain miserable we invariably get the advice to just "think positively!" Sometimes it's difficult to figure out exactly what that means.

Perhaps at times we would prefer to wallow. Surely there must be some merit in wallowing. Indeed there may be, (time heals most wounds) however, at some point we have to pick ourselves up and move on.

In order to do so, we must change our mindset or attitude from a non-productive one, into one that is positive and progressive. Of course, we can't be in denial or adopt a Pollyannaish, rose-coloured glasses way of looking at the world.

Negative feelings and circumstances do exist and often serve as an indication that something is not working or needs to be attended to. In such cases we must employ positive thinking and use it as a strategy for interpreting everything that happens to us in a useful, constructive way in order to make our lives work.

Here are some tips on how to develop a positive thinking mindset and how to incorporate it into your daily awareness:

- Accept that you are here to grow and evolve

Life doesn't always go smoothly. Not everything is meant to be a joyride or exercise in pleasure. Life's lessons can be difficult, but are more so if you approach them with avoidance and apprehension. If you see them as opportunities to become stronger, wiser and more resilient, you are thinking positively and productively.

- Learn to turn lemons into lemonade

Look for the lessons to be learned in every situation. Instead of feeling sorry for yourself when things don't go your way, do what you can to make the best of it. You can learn to avoid falling in the same traps, making the same mistakes and by doing so, be the better for it.

As James Joyce said:

"A man's errors are his portals of discovery."

- Believe in yourself

Know that you have what it takes to succeed. Your dreams and goals are an indication where your talents lie and where your true potential is. Needless to say, you must develop your inherent gifts; however, recognise that you have a unique contribution to make. You're one of a kind.

"Magic is believing in yourself, if you can do that, you can make anything happen." *Johann Wolfgang von Goethe*

- Acquire perseverance

When you possess a positive thinking mindset you never give

up. You pursue your dreams, goals and objectives with everything you've got and you don't settle for anything less. That's not to say you won't have roadblocks and various setbacks along the way. It just means that you won't let them stop you!

"Our greatest glory is not in never failing, but in rising up every time we fail."

- Look for inspiration and support

Read about and study the triumphs of others. Many successful people have gone through challenging circumstances to get where they are. Learning about their trials and tribulations can motivate and inspire you to achieve what you desire to achieve. To help you stay positive and focused, garner support from family and friends.

So the next time some well-meaning person tells you to think positively, just smile back confidently and let them know that it's part of your everyday, productive mindset.

Good Communication Skills – Key to Any Success

Good communication skills are a key to success in life, work, and relationships. Without effective communication, a message can turn into error, misunderstanding, frustration or even disaster by being misinterpreted or poorly delivered.

Communication is the process by which we exchange information between individuals or groups of people. It's a process where we try, as clearly and accurately as we can, to convey our thoughts, intentions and objectives.

It is successful only when both the sender and the receiver understand the same information.

Although it's become increasingly important to have good communication skills in this highly informational and technological environment, many individuals continue to struggle. When they are unable to communicate effectively, they are held back both in their careers and in social and personal relationships.

How can We Acquire Good Communication Skills to be More Effective?

The Important steps:

1. Know what you want to say and why

Understand clearly the purpose and intent of your message. Know to whom you are communicating and why. Consider any barriers you may encounter such as cultural differences or situational circumstances (gender, age or economic biases). Ask yourself what outcome you want to achieve and the impression you want to leave.

2. How will you say it?

We're all aware by now that it's not always what you say, but how you say it. Begin by making eye contact. You inspire trust and confidence when you look a person in the eyes when you speak. Second, be aware of your body language since it can say so much more than your words.

By standing with arms easily at your side you tell others that you are approachable and open to hearing what they have to say. If, instead, your arms are crossed and shoulders hunched, it suggests disinterest or unwillingness to communicate. Good posture and an approachable stance help make even difficult communication flow more smoothly. Make sure you speak in a cooperative, non-adversarial tone. Be non-judgemental.

3. Listen

Communication is a two-way street. After you've said what you have to say, stop, listen and look for feedback and clues of comprehension. While the person is responding avoid any impulses to cut them off or listen only for the end of the sentence so that you can blurt out more ideas or thoughts that come to your mind. Respectfully give them your full attention. When they are finished, to ensure that your message has been clearly and correctly understood, ask open questions and encourage discussion. Fine-tune your message if necessary.

4. Reach understanding, agreement or consensus

Once you have had to opportunity to discuss your message and the feedback to it, re-visit the purpose of the interchange. Have you reached common ground, solved a problem or clarified your position? If the purpose was to teach or instruct, have you accomplished your goal?

To communicate well is to understand and be understood. Make sure that your message has been received as intended and that any questions or concerns have been alleviated. You can even agree to disagree. There are no guarantees that your communication efforts will be meet with total compliance and agreement. As long as you understand each other, are cordial and respectful, you can still have a successful exchange.

Helpful Tips for Developing Good Communication Skills

- To obtain a better command of the English language (or any other language), expand your vocabulary by reading and writing more. Look up words you're not familiar with. The better you are able to express yourself, the better your ability to communicate.
- Practice your listening skills. Be considerate of other

speakers by waiting until they are done before stating your views. Process what has being said before responding.

- Learn to understand and appreciate opposing points of view by being open-minded and making an effort to see things from others' perspective. It will in turn, gain you more cooperation and understanding.
- Avoid trying to communicate when in an emotional state. You lose objectivity and may say something inappropriate or regrettable. Take time to think your position through before speaking.
- Join an organisation such as Toastmasters that encourages you to develop a variety of communication skills, as well as the opportunity to meet new and interesting people.

When you take the time to acquire and hone good communication skills you open yourself up to better relationships, more career opportunities and increased self-confidence. You also reach higher levels of mutual understanding and cooperation while achieving your goals with even greater success. All new skills take time to refine, however, with effort and practice you can develop good, even exceptional, communication skills.

■■■

Chapter 7

Personal Development Techniques

The Benefits of Practicing Mindfulness

Mindfulness was originally developed in the Buddhist traditions of Asia, but today is used as a technique in which a person becomes intentionally and non-judgementally aware of their thoughts and actions in the present moment.

It is the practice of being aware of ourselves without getting caught up in thinking about the past or worrying about the future.

One of the big challenges we face in this fast-paced, ever changing world is to be present in our own lives. We tend to get so caught up in the frenzy of what's going on around us that we often overlook what's happening in the moment. Why is this a problem?

It's a problem because on a day-to-day basis it causes us stress and strain, wear and tear and becomes detrimental to our physical and emotional health.

Likewise, left unchecked the mind can wander and unleash

all kinds of negative thoughts and emotions including anger, cravings, jealousy, depression and countless others. However, practicing being mindful can harness and manage those thoughts and promote self-awareness and inner calm. Researchers who have studied the effects of those who practice mindfulness found that the subjects generally experience less negative emotions, are more happy and optimistic, and have more even left-right brain activity.

How to Put it to Practice?

1. **Start by making the effort**: Make a commitment to change the habits of rushing, functioning haphazardly and not paying attention. Notice areas where you are not being mindful.
2. **Slow down:** Take a deep breath before beginning an activity, no matter what it is, and focus on the process.
3. **Observe yourself:** If the present moment involves stress, observe your thoughts and emotions and how they affect your body. Notice when your thoughts are distracting you from the present moment.
4. **Practice:** Get practise being mindful by performing a task you usually do impatiently or unconsciously, such as brushing your teeth, and do it mindfully.

The Benefits

- Helps you stay focused on what's happening in the present.
- Helps reduce fear/anxiety and promotes feelings of being in control.
- Helps prevent being eating by your making healthier food choices when you pay attention to what you eat.
- Helps you more fully experience and enjoy what you are doing.

- Helps you make better decisions since you are more present and have the opportunity to assess.
- Bolsters your immune system by allowing you to be more relaxed and deliberate.
- Reduces stress since you're in tune with your thoughts and your body.
- Helps you enhance your social and communication skills by becoming a better, more empathetic listener.

Being mindful doesn't mean you'll never be in a hurry, have upsetting thoughts and emotions, or not be able to do more than one thing at once. It merely means that you'll be doing them all more consciously.

You will have more insight and awareness of your choices and your ability to make better ones will be enhanced. To have a calmer, more enjoyable existence, make the commitment today to be more mindful and aware of everything you do.

Emotional Freedom Technique Can Change Your Life

Emotional Freedom Technique can change your life. More people are taking responsibility for their own well-being than ever before. As a result there are self-help modalities available to suit everyone's needs. The modern energy therapies, which have come to the fore in the last two decades, are favourites because they are simple and very effective.

One of the best energy therapies out there is EFT, Emotional Freedom Technique. EFT is simple, powerful and versatile. It addresses all types of emotional and physical issues. Since it manipulates the body's energy system, whilst simultaneously using mind focus to address a particular issue it can also be used for general problem-solving in business.

How Emotional Freedom Technique Heals Emotional and Physical Problems

It is an irrefutable fact that our thinking directly affects our well-being. Negative thinking creates low energy levels and positive thinking produces higher energy levels.

EFT works on the premise that persistent negative thinking causes a lowering of general energy levels ultimately disrupting the free flow of energy in the body. The disruptions caused to the body's energy system eventually manifest as emotional or physical problems.

EFT uses a form of needle free acupuncture together with mind focus to address any issue. You tap on a small number of meridian points on the body and face, whilst repeating aloud an "affirmation" phrase related to the issue you are addressing.

Tapping on the meridian points opens up the energy channels in the body. This enables the energy to start flowing freely again and releases negativity at the same time.

This process works very quickly: One round of tapping, as we call it, takes one minute. Typically you would tap three to five rounds, depending on the severity of your symptoms. Within this short time you will notice a sudden increase of your energy levels.

An EFT technique developed, combining the EFT modality with breathing techniques. This is a very powerful combination and is particularly useful if you're suffering from anxiety or phobias of any kind.

Use EFT for Anything

The beauty of EFT is its immense versatility. Once you have learned the basics you can use it to release negative emotions and obtain relief from physical symptoms as well as manifest positive changes in your life. EFT is the perfect tool to speed up goal manifesting, like creating more money, improving your relationships or eating healthier, to name but a few examples.

EFT also works brilliantly with children. Children have fewer inhibitions then us grown ups and they love the off beat approach and creativity of EFT. They also often bring a humour to the therapy, which facilitates the healing process. Humour actually is an important part of EFT. It is to encourage people to take a lighthearted approach to the entire process and not to take themselves and their problems too seriously. This approach often works wonders. It defuses old, longstanding issues with laughter in no time at all.

If you are looking to improve your life, please check out EFT and the many ways in which it can help you. EFT really has the potential to enrich your life beyond your wildest dreams.

Affirmations – How to Make Them Real?

There has been some speculation as to whether using affirmations is helpful in pursuing personal development and setting goals.

In a word, yes.

Affirmations are repeated positive statements designed to bring about a desired result. The repetitious aspect is meant to influence and trigger the subconscious mind into positive action.

It's no surprise that on a daily basis we often unconsciously repeat negative statements to ourselves about different situations in our lives. In doing so we often bring about the undesirable circumstance itself.

We might say to ourselves "I can't do this", "I'm not good enough for that" or "this will never work".

Needless to say, our proclamations become self-fulfilling prophesies.

The reverse can also be true.

If we were to turn the negative statements we frequently utter into positive ones, we would bring about more favourable outcomes.

Take Muhammad Ali as an example. Who hasn't heard his famous declaration?

"I am the greatest, I said that even before I knew I was."

Muhammad Ali

Is there any question in anyone's mind that Ali's repetition of that phrase helped him achieve the status of being "the greatest"?

Another one of his famous maxims was "I float like a butterfly, sting like a bee". I'm sure his opponents shuddered at the mere mention of it.

Another interesting illustration for the effectiveness of affirmations comes from the auto suggestion work of Emile Coué the French psychologist and pharmacist who introduced the now famous phrase:

"Every day, in every way, I'm getting better and better".

As a tool for self-improvement, he recommended that we begin each day by stating it firmly and convincingly.

Coué felt that, as stated in his "Law of Concentrated Attention", whenever attention is concentrated on an idea over and over again, it spontaneously tends to realise itself. In working with his patients he utilised this law to help them build their self-image.

Since then affirmations have also been used in cognitive therapy and found to work quite well. Needless to say there's no magic to it and there are limitations.

Certainly you wouldn't make an affirmation that is unrealistic or makes no sense. Ultimately they're meant to serve as another helpful tool in furthering your personal development.

The Benefits

- When used properly, they can change your attitude and behaviours.
- Can change negative thinking into positive.
- Can help you stay focused.
- Can help you relax and release tension.
- They can motivate you to achieve your goals.

Tips on Use:

1. Make up special, meaningful phrases in your own descriptive words. It makes them more credible and therefore more effective.
2. Write them down so you remember what they are and are able to use them over and over again.
3. Always state them in the positive, for example say, "I am good at this", instead of "I will not be bad at this".
4. Find a specific time and a quite place and repeat them at least twice daily.

5. State them with conviction, enthusiasm and desire.
6. Live them. Practice what you affirm.

As you can see employing positive phrases and assertions in your personal development can serve as a useful and productive tool. Anything you can believe, you can achieve.

Visualisation: A Key to Achieving Your Goals

Visualisation is an important personal development tool. Just as affirmations can help you motivate yourself and focus better to achieve your goals so can using visualisation or mental imagery.

Although it has only become really popular as a personal development technique since the late seventies and early eighties, we as humans have been using it since the beginning of time.

Whenever we have an idea or notion to do something we visualise it first. For instance, if we're hungry and want to eat we picture different food possibilities; whether we want to cook a meal or go out to eat, and whether or not we want company at our meal. When we have a function to attend we picture what type of outfit to wear and where we might shop for it.

What is Visualisation?

It is the use of the imagination through pictures or mental imagery to create visions of what we want in our lives and how to make them happen. Along with focus and emotion it becomes a powerful, creative tool that helps us achieve what we want in life.

Used correctly it can bring about self-improvement, maintain good health, help you perform well in sports, and accomplish your goals in life.

In sports, mental imagery is often used by athletes to improve their skills by picturing the achievement of a specific feat, such as hitting or shooting a ball, skiing a hill, swimming or running a race, among other things.

Using it as a technique invariably results in a much better performance and outcome. This also holds true in business or in life such as in delivering a speech, asking for a raise or any other situation that requires preparedness and forethought.

How Does it Work?

Visualisation or mental imagery works because when you imagine yourself performing perfectly and doing exactly what you want, you physiologically create neural patterns in your brain, just as if you had physically performed the action. The thought can stimulate the nervous system in the same way as the actual event does.

Performing or rehearsing an event in the mind trains it and creates the neural patterns to teach our muscles to do exactly what we want them to do.

In the case of competitive sports, not only are exceptional physical skills required, but so is a strong mental game. Most coaches preach that sports are 90% mental and only 10% physical. That's why so many athletes train in visualisation or mental imagery along with their physical routines.

To be effective, like any skill, mental imagery needs to be practiced regularly. The four elements to mental imagery are relaxation, realism, regularity and reinforcement.

Ways in Which to Use Visualisation

Success: See yourself performing skills at a high level, achieving your goals, being who you want to be and living the life you want.

To motivate: Envision yourself achieving your goals vividly to remind yourself of your objective and what you need to do to reach it. Many athletes, actors, and singers "see" and "feel" themselves performing a routine, programme, or play perfectly before they actually do it.

To familiarise or set the stage for a performance/event: Mental imagery can be used effectively to familiarise yourself with the surroundings before an event, such as a competition site, a racetrack, a stage or a difficult play or routine prior to a competition.

To do a run-through: Athletes and performers often do a complete mental run through of the key elements of their routines. This helps them focus, eliminate some pre-performance jitters and be more comfortable. It also serves as a warm-up or mini rehearsal.

You can use visualisation for anything and everything that you want to prepare for in advance. It helps you be more comfortable and perform at a higher level no matter what. It's a great way to rehearse and prepare for any kind of event or situation.

How to Visualise What you Want:

1. Go somewhere quiet and private where you won't be disturbed. Close your eyes and think of the goal, mood, new behaviour or skill, you want to acquire.
2. Take several deep breaths and relax.
3. Visualise the object or situation you desire in your mind as clearly and with as much detail as you can.
4. Add emotion, feeling, and your senses to your vision.
5. Practice it at least twice a day for about 10 minutes each time.

6. Persevere until you succeed.
7. Maintain positive thoughts and a good attitude throughout.

The Benefits of Visualisation

- Helps you focus better in order to achieve your goals
- Inspires and motivates you.
- Helps you improve in a sport or skill.
- Can be used to rehearse and then acquire new, positive behaviours.
- Can boost your mood by using positive, pleasant imagery to alter negative emotions.
- Helps build self-confidence.

How to Think Critically and Problem Solving?

The quote on the right by *Jean De La Bruyere* may seem a bit radical, however, according to the premise of cognitive psychology, what you think is what you feel.

While many people believe that your feelings precede, or are independent of your thoughts, the truth is that your feelings are products of your thoughts.

This revelation can be both daunting and liberating.

Daunting because it makes us responsible for our attitudes and liberating because we have the power to choose our perspective, mood and thoughts.

When we are aware that we can choose and direct our thinking, we realise that we have the ability to better control the circumstances of our lives, improve our decision-making processes and generally live more productive lives.

This in no way suggests that we need downplay the many feelings and emotions we as humans enjoy, it's a simply a way for us to manage and balance them with our cognitive abilities.

We are thinking critically and in a problem-solving mindset when we:

- Rely on reason rather than emotion
- Evaluate a broad range of viewpoints and open mind to alternative interpretations
- Accept new evidence, explanations and findings
- Are willing to reassess information
- Can put aside personal prejudices and biases
- Consider all reasonable possibilities
- Avoid hasty judgements

Like any other skill, learning to think critically or problem-solving takes time, perseverance and practice. Knowing which steps to take and how to apply them helps us master the process.

Steps to Critical Thinking as it Relates to Problem-Solving:

1. Identify the Problem

The first task is to determine if a problem exists. Sometimes when you think this point through, you may come to the conclusion that there really isn't a problem, just a misunderstanding. If that's the case, fine. If not, and you determine that there is indeed a problem, you need to identify exactly what it is.

2. Analyse the problem, look at it from different angles

Once you've determined the problem, analyse it by looking at it from a variety of perspectives. Is it solvable? Is it real or perceived? Can you solve it alone or do you need help? Sometimes by looking at it from many angles you can come up with a resolution right away. You may also reveal a bias or narrow point of view that needs to be broadened.

3. Brainstorm and come up with a several possible solutions

Problems can be solved in many ways. Brainstorm a list of several possible solutions. Put down anything that comes to mind and then go over the list and narrow it down to the best possibilities. Having several viable options leads to obtaining the best results.

4. Decide which solution fits the situation best

Go over your list of possible solutions. Different situations call for different solutions. Quite often what works in one situation, may not work in a similar one. Take time to determine what will work best for the problem at hand. One solution usually does not fit all.

5. Take action

Implement your solution. Every problem has a solution; even if it may be to accept the situation, and move on.

Instead of approaching problems and challenges as insurmountable obstacles, we can view them as opportunities to hone our self-confidence and self-worth.

Thinking critically not only helps us handle future challenges more skilfully, it also broadens our life experience and helps us gain perspective.

Keys to Making a Good Decision

There are important steps and keys to making a good decision.

Good or sound decision-making is necessary for living life productively and efficiently.

All of us are confronted with various decisions to make on a daily basis. Some are small and of minor consequence while others are huge and potentially life-changing. Some are simple and obvious choices; others are more difficult and painstaking.

For those that are complex and difficult to make, there is a process we can follow to help us come up with a good solution.

The Keys to Making a Good Decision

1. Identify the decision to be made as well as the objectives or outcome you want to achieve.
2. Do your homework. Gather as many facts and as much information you can to assess your options.
3. Brainstorm and come up with several possible choices. Determine if the options are compatible with your values, interests and abilities.
4. Weigh the probabilities or possible outcomes. In other words, what's the worst that can happen? What will happen if I do A, B or C and can I live with the consequences?
5. Make a list of the pros and cons. Prioritise which considerations are very important to you, and which are less so. Sometimes when you match the pros against the cons you may find them dramatically lopsided.
6. Solicit opinions and obtain feedback from those you trust or have had a similar situation to contend with. There may be some points you haven't considered.
7. Make the decision and monitor your results. Make sure you obtain the desired outcome.

Points to Consider

Certainly there is no guarantees that a decision will be correct and so you must be prepared to take risks.

By the same token, look for the opportunities. If you make a mistake, view it as an opportunity to learn what didn't work and why. Many times decisions are reversible and you can change your mind.

On occasion you might discover things in hindsight that may have affected your decision had you known about them earlier. This is normal and typical but should not stall your decision-making process.

If you've done everything you can to make a good decision and still can't make up your mind, do not delay making an important decision for fear that you don't know enough or will make the wrong choice.

Sometimes people become so paralysed with the fear of making a wrong decision that they panic and lose sight of what they're trying to accomplish.

When that happens it hinders making a good decision. Likewise, try not to second-guess yourself. In the end it too undermines what you're trying to accomplish.

When all is said and done, all you can do is do the best with what you have to work with. If all else fails go with your gut feeling. Quite often it may be all you have to go by.

Expand Your Comfort Zone

From a psychological standpoint your comfort zone is an artificial mental boundary within which you maintain a sense of security and out of which you experience great discomfort.

For the most part your comfort zone is a reflection of your self-image and how you think and expect things should be.

When you are in an uncomfortable situation, or one that doesn't fit your expectations, you usually do whatever you can to make yourself comfortable again.

For many people, even if they are unhappy or unfulfilled, their natural inclination is to stay within the comfort zone simply because it is familiar and safe.

Many stay in jobs, relationships, and situations that have long since lost their relevance only because they are afraid of the unknown. The truth is that security does not reside in anything outside of ourselves; instead, it lies within us.

Unfortunately, if you choose to remain in your comfort zone you will never find out what your true potential is or what you are capable of achieving. Nor can you really succeed at anything without venturing out of the comfort of your safety net.

If, however, you make the decision to move beyond the circumstances, people, and experiences you are familiar with, you move out of your comfort zone and onto the path of personal development. It is a path that forces you to stretch yourself, push your limits and become more than you were.

Of course you don't have to do anything extraordinarily out of character, like climbing Mt. Everest or swimming the English Channel if you have no inclination or desire for it. Stretching yourself does not have to be that extreme.

Anyone who takes a new subject in school, learns a new language, takes up a new sport or starts a new job, operates out of their comfort zone in the beginning.

Here are some other things you can do:

1. Break from a routine or habit you've had for a long time and find a different, perhaps better way to do it.
2. If you're typically a sedentary person take a break from reading or the computer and find a physical activity you can enjoy and partake in.

   If you're normally very active, learn to wind down, read or relax.
3. Read a book, watch a movie or listen to music in a genre you're not familiar with. If you usually read mysteries, try reading an inspiring biography, if you like action movies, try a romantic comedy, if you just listen to rock, try some jazz music.
4. If happen to be a shy person and have trouble speaking in front of people, join a group of experts who encourage you to speak in public by using positive and helpful techniques.

   The more practice you get, the more comfortable you'll be and the better you will feel about yourself.
5. Go to an ethnic restaurant and try a dish from a culture different from your own. It will stimulate your taste buds and possibly open up a whole new cuisine.
6. Volunteer at the downtown mission or soup kitchen for a day and realise how comfortable your life really is, while helping someone at the same time.

Benefits of Expanding your Comfort Zone:

- Enhances your enjoyment and experience of life
- Stimulates brain activity and therefore boosts your mental health

- Increases self-confidence
- Makes you more resilient
- Helps prevent getting stuck in a rut or becoming depressed
- Challenges you to improve yourself
- Prevents atrophy

Stretching yourself and expanding your comfort zone is an important part of personal development. Each step advances you to the next level and keeps you on the path of self-improvement.

■■■

Chapter 8

Positive Personal Development Habits

Invest in Your Personal Development

When you invest in your personal development you take responsibility for your life, your circumstances and your happiness. You become the agent, the doer, and the effecter.

If, on the other hand, you sit back and don't make the effort to take charge of your life you set yourself up for events to affect you. If you're unprepared and not proactive you will end up reacting to, rather than affecting what is going on around you.

It would be like being on a boat that springs a leak. If you haven't prepared for the possibility, you'll be scrambling around bailing out water, panicking, and hoping you don't sink. If, however, you had anticipated this could happen, you have the proper tools handy, you fix the leak, secure your vessel and proceed with your journey.

Two very different responses to the same obstacle.

So it is with life. Nothing is guaranteed or always goes smoothly as planned. Not your job, your relationships, your health or anything else. Given that uncertainty, in order to make your life work, you have to plan, prepare and bring your best game (the best you).

Where do you start?

Once again you start with yourself . You invest in your personal development and work on being the best that you can be.

When you do, everything else comes together in seemingly effortless fashion – your relationships, your work, your home life, and your over-all sense of well-being. This doesn't mean that there aren't challenges and obstacles. There always are. It just means that you are better equipped to handle them.

How do you go about it?

Devise a personal development action plan or checklist to follow. It can be flexible and serve as a guide or outline for what you want to accomplish. Write it in journal or chart format so you can monitor your progress.

For example:

Under Health

- Will incorporate a new exercise into routine. (If you don't have a routine this is a good time to start one.)
- Will cut down on fat/food intake and try eating a new fruit or vegetable each month.
- Will drink an extra glass of water each day.
- Will go to bed a half hour earlier.
- Will cut down on junk food.

Under Intellectual Development

- Will read a new book each week (biweekly or monthly).
- Will go to the art gallery, theatre or symphony/concert once a month.
- Will listen to a new musical genre or artist.
- Will read about a different philosopher or literary figure once a month.

Under Emotional and Spiritual

- Will learn to meditate, or learn a relaxation or deep breathing technique.
- Will take time for myself to rejuvenate, contemplate and connect.
- Will make a point of spending some quality time for family and friends.
- Will visualise and use affirmations to get into the positive thinking habit.

You can devise any kind of plan or schedule that suits your tastes and needs. The important part is to make a conscious decision to actively engage in personal development. Always be willing to stretch yourself, keep an open mind and learn new things.

Benefits of Investing in Your Personal Development:

- Be proactive and affect change rather than merely react to or be at the mercy of it.
- Enjoy a sense of mastery and accomplishment.
- Be better able to maintain control of your reactions and emotions.

- Better clarify and define your goals.
- Live life more consciously, purposefully and deliberately.
- Be more focused and centred.
- Acquire more self-awareness, self-trust and self-confidence.
- Be more genuine and true to yourself.

Take the time to invest in yourself by developing all aspects of your being – physically, mentally, emotionally and spiritually. To be the best you can be is to live life to the fullest!

Personal Development and Human Potential

How can we define personal development and how does it relate to human potential?

Personal development is not measured by financial, social or external success. Instead it is determined by our efforts to develop our intellectual, physical and spiritual aspects in order to reach our full human potential.

In the process of developing ourselves, we also strive to express our talents and abilities in order to enrich and benefit others.

Unfortunately, in today's instant gratification culture, there has been an unhealthy trend attempting to convince people to buy into "get rich quick" (substitute thin, beautiful, fit, etc.) schemes.

It implies that if you are rich enough, thin enough, or beautiful enough, you will be a happy. Instead of encouraging legitimate personal growth and development, these schemes and false claims work against it.

We have all read about and heard countless tales of lottery winners attaining massive riches only to be broke not long after their windfalls. We have also seen beautiful, rich, and influential entertainment stars end their own unhappy lives in spite of their outward success.

There are no "quick fixes" or short cuts to personal development.

It is a deliberate, disciplined process achieved by reflection, introspection and self-awareness.

Personal Development and the Human Potential Movement

The emphasis on personal development began to rise in the world in 1960's with the Human Potential Movement that had its roots in existentialism and humanistic psychology.

Its purpose was to promote the idea that humans can experience an exceptional quality of life filled with happiness, creativity, and fulfilment when they strive to reach their potential.

Abraham Maslow, a humanistic psychologist, put forth the idea that self-actualisation (the fulfilment of self through reaching one's potential) is the highest expression of a human's life.

In his research Maslow found that self-actualised people were those who are creative and spontaneous, possess a good sense of humour and are able to tolerate uncertainty.

They have an appreciation for what life has to offer, a deep concern for others and are able to enjoy close, meaningful, personal relationships.

He advocated a list of behaviours that he felt lead to self-actualisation.

These behaviours include:

- Maintain the curiosity, attention and wonder you had as a child.
- Be open-minded and try new things.
- Be honest and be willing to risk unpopularity if you disagree with others.
- Use your intelligence and work hard at whatever you do.
- Find out who you are, what you want and what's important to you.
- Don't be afraid to open yourself up to new experiences.
- Take responsibility for your iife and your actions.

Humanistic psychology emphasises the importance of attending to and developing the "whole" person or those aspects of ourselves that make us human – the physical, the emotional, the intellectual and the spiritual.

To be your "true self" means to be it and take responsibility for it on all of these levels.

Personal development is therefore, the process of striving to be the best that you can be in order to reach and realise your full potential. It is a journey of self-discovery, self-improvement and self-realisation.

Overcoming Fear

Overcoming fear, whatever it happens to be, can be challenging, but when conquered, very liberating.

Fear is an emotion experienced in anticipation of some specific pain or danger and is usually accompanied by a desire to flee or fight. It can be real or imagined.

It is certainly not always a bad thing. When it serves as a warning signal for impending danger or a life-threatening situation, it is necessary and life preserving. If we didn't feel it in certain situations we wouldn't react appropriately and we'd put ourselves at great risk.

If a fear is imagined or irrational it can be paralysing and hold us back from living life fully and productively. Many imagined fears such as the fear of rejection, looking foolish, or failure are the types of fears we must learn to manage and overcome. If we let them control our lives we would never venture forth and become all that we can be.

There are, of course, some fears that our having them, or not, doesn't affect our lives. For example, if someone has a fear of public speaking yet has no need, intention or desire to speak publicly; trying to conquer the fear is of no consequence.

There is really no motivation to work on conquering it. If, on the other hand, the fear of public speaking will hold them back in their career, or getting ahead in any way, then it's time to work on it.

Strategies for Overcoming Fear

1. **Acknowledge the fear:** Whether it's imagined or real, the first step in overcoming fear is to admit that it exists. We all have fears, it's human nature. Denying or ignoring them doesn't make them go away.
2. **Analyse it:** Where does it come from? Is it real or imagined? Can it be put in a different context? For instance if you think it through to it's logical conclusion what's the worst that can happen to you? Once you've determined what that might be, ask yourself if you can deal with or

overcome it. More often than not, once you go through the process of analysing it, the fear isn't as scary as you originally imagined.

3. **Face it:** Allow yourself to feel it, and then do it anyway. Act in spite of your fear and treat is as a challenge for personal growth and opportunity to become stronger.
4. **Be persistent:** Do the thing you fear over and over again. By doing it repeatedly it loses its power over you and you become less vulnerable to it.
5. **Develop courage:** Sometimes the answer may not be to conquer a particular fear; it may be to develop courage. If you focus too much on any one fear instead of trying to build courage, you may, in fact, intensify it. By developing courage you build self-confidence and resistance. Also, by developing courage, you build a healthy approach towards all fear.

As Mark Twain said:

"Courage is resistance to fear, mastery of fear, not absence of fear."

Here is list of top nine fears according to Forbes.com:

1. Fear of bugs (especially spiders), mice, snakes, bats
2. Fear of heights
3. Fear of water (drowning)
4. Fear of public transportation
5. Fear of storms
6. Fear of closed spaces
7. Fear of tunnels and bridges
8. Fear of crowds
9. Fear of public speaking

How many on this list can you count as your own? Decide which ones you may want to work on and overcome your fears.

Tips to Help You Manage Change

Nothing stays the same.

Today, in this fast-paced, unpredictable world, not only is change inevitable, it is happening more quickly than ever before. It is becoming a way of life.

It's not enough that we have to deal with the normal personal changes that we all go through in life, but these days we also have broader issues to contend with such as the global economy, the domestic economy (job loss, company closures), the environment, technology, and changing cultural values.

As challenging and difficult as it may be, and as resistant we are to it, we have to learn to manage change. Most of us are comfortable with the known and uncomfortable with the unknown.

It is in our best interests, however, to learn to accept change and welcome its challenges. We can come to terms with the fact that it can actually be good for us since it helps us develop and encourages us to grow.

Here are some helpful tips and strategies for change management:

1. Take care of yourself

Eat a balanced diet, exercise, get enough rest. Take time to relax. When you are healthy, you are better equipped and in a better frame of mind to handle anything.

2. Be open and flexible

Knowing that change can occur at any time helps you accept and adjust to it when does happen. Be able to let go of expectations that no longer fit what is currently going on in the world. Even though most of us prefer to settle into comfortable routines, realise that your present routine may only be temporary.

3. Stay positive and put it in perspective

We all have the ability to control our inner and emotional responses to whatever happens, our attitudes towards it, and how we choose to deal with it.

Look for the positive outcomes of change. How you react to it can often determine the outcome.

4. Take control of your life

Use your critical thinking skills. We know some change is forthcoming. What can you do in advance to help yourself in the transition? Make a list of options. Determine the best approaches. Take charge of your thoughts and actions.

5. Make changes

Become the change agent. Sometimes we are forced into making changes because we allow ourselves to get stuck in a routine or lifestyle that is no longer working for us.

If, however, we anticipate it and become active rather than reactive, we can take control of the situation. We can look at where we need to make adjustments and then take action. Doing so can prevent the stress and anxiety that accompany unexpected change.

Change in life is inevitable. Rather than fear or try avoid it, our best course of action is to accept it, meet it head on and allow it to be a positive, constructive force in our lives.

Positive Habits to Develop

Here are some positive habits that you can consider incorporating into your routine.

Quite often we get so caught up in day-to-day activities that we get distracted from thinking about and developing little positive habits that could make the difference between having an okay day and a upbeat, positive day.

Some of them may seem so simple and obvious that we don't even think of implementing them regularly.

1. Start the day with a positive mind-set

Upon awakening make the commitment to face the day and whatever it brings with a positive frame of mind. Prepare yourself for the fact that everything may not go smoothly or as planned, and be willing to handle any challenges you're faced with (we know there will be some).

2. Practice Gratitude

Be grateful for and focus on the good things you have in your life. Many of us get in the habit of sweating the "small stuff" and let it get in the way of appreciating the important things - family, friends, good health, freedom and the many opportunities we enjoy.

When we let that happen it downplays the fact that we really do have much to be grateful for.

3. Learn something new

Make a conscious effort to keep your brain active and functioning at optimum levels. Learn a new vocabulary word or a new piece of information as often as you can. It will keep you sharp and alert.

4. Have a good laugh

Read the comics or tell a joke just to loosen things up. It will help relieve stress, keep things light and change your perspective.

5. Smile at someone

When you walk through the office, down the street or are in a store, make it a point to smile at someone to acknowledge them. It will make you both feel good. We're usually so preoccupied and caught up in activity that we don't take time to notice those around us.

6. Give a heartfelt compliment

If you notice someone at school/work that has a new hairdo or outfit and looks especially good, or has just given a good presentation, don't hold back give them a compliment. Everyone enjoys positive feedback.

7. Tell your spouse, family member or friend how much you appreciate them

Just as we enjoy a nice compliment now and then, it makes us feel good to know a loved one appreciates us. Quite often we take those we are closest to for granted.

8. Perform an act of kindness

Do something nice just for the sake of doing it. Help an elderly person lift or carry a parcel. Clear the table after a meal if it's not your normal routine. Offer to take your neighbour's kids to the park or the show along with yours. It generates and promotes good will.

9. Be a better listener

Take the time to listen to another's point of view. Even if you don't agree with what they are saying, try to put yourself in their place and understand where they're coming from.

10. Take 10-15 minutes quiet time

Give yourself a break. You deserve time to reflect and regroup too. Even a little 15-minute catnap can be surprisingly refreshing and rejuvenating.

These positive habits can be incorporated into your routine at whatever intervals are comfortable for you. To be aware of them and to practice them regularly will help make each day more pleasant for you and those around you.

Character Traits Worth Developing

It is a wonderful set of principles to live by and which can never steer you wrong.

1. **Be Honest:** Tell the truth; be sincere; don't mislead or withhold key information in relationships of trust; don't steal.
2. **Demonstrate integrity:** Stand up for your beliefs about right and wrong; be your best self; resist social pressure to do wrong.
3. **Keep promises:** Keep your word and honour your commitments; pay your debts and return what you borrow.
4. **Be loyal:** Stand by family, friends, employers, community and country; don't talk about people behind their backs.
5. **Be responsible:** Think before you act; consider consequences; be accountable and "take your medicine".
6. **Pursue excellence:** Do your best with what you have; don't quit easily.
7. **Be kind and caring:** Show you care through generosity and compassion; don't be selfish or mean.
8. **Treat all people with respect:** Be courteous and polite;

judge all people on their merits; be tolerant, appreciative and accepting of individual differences.

9. Be fair: Treat all people fairly; be open-minded; listen to others and try to understand what they are saying and feeling.
10. Be a good citizen: Obey the law and respect authority; vote, volunteer your efforts; protect the environment.

These principles are also an excellent basis for developing a Personal Value System. As mentioned, you can't go wrong by using them to guide your actions. They can help you develop solid friendships, a good career and a foundation of good reputation and integrity.

■■■